£7-99

Moreton Morrell Site

Arkle

The Classic Story of a Champion

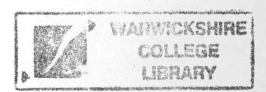

Arkle

The Classic Story of a Champion

IVOR HERBERT

AURUM PRESS

This edition first published in Great Britain
2003 by Aurum Press Ltd
25 Bedford Avenue, London WC1B 3AT

First published 1966 by Pelham Books

Revised edition published 1975 by William Luscombe Ltd

A catalogue record for this book is available from the British Library.

ISBN 1 85410 912 X

3 5 7 9 10 8 6 4 2
2003 2005 2007 2006 2004

Printed by Bookmarque, Croydon

To
the late Tom Dreaper,
Trainer, and his Jockey, the late Pat Taaffe,
this revised biography of his great horse
is dedicated
with my respect

ILLUSTRATIONS

INTRODUCTION

IN THE NEARLY FORTY YEARS since Arkle ran his last race no steeple-chaser has come within shouting distance of his supremacy. Good horses have run and won since the 27th December, 1966, (as they did before 1962 when he began his complete domination of the British and Irish steeplechasing landscapes) but no other horse has been even in the same league. In his lifetime handicaps were constructed two-fold: one with Arkle in it (he with the maximum, the rest usually on the minimum weight); and the other with a normal range relating to ordinary horses.

Since that grey day at Kempton when he split one third of his pedal-bone and ran nearly three miles in mounting pain, many good horses have raced, beating one another as weights and conditions altered, all comfortably capable of being lumped together in normal handicaps.

Two seasons after Arkle's last race and before the official announcement of his retirement in October, 1968 his stable companion Fort Leney won 'chasing's single classic, the Cheltenham Gold Cup. And Arkle was at that time officially rated by the Irish handicapper no less than three stone superior to Fort Leney. Forty-two pounds better than the latest Gold Cup winner! As the mind boggles, the handicapper gives it another whirl: he declares that not even that difference could bring together that very good horse and the incomparable Arkle.

We are dealing with a phenomenon. The degree by which Arkle soared above other horses is no more explicable than the occasional explosion in the human race of a genius. Men like Shakespeare, Beethoven, Churchill had no discernible reason in their heredity or appearance which lofted them not only high above their contemporaries, but above those who in their fields went before or followed after.

Arkle possessed an athlete's physical attributes: power, speed, judgement, balance, a quick eye, stamina and the ability to learn, absorb and then react instinctively. Other good horses have had these talents, or most of them, in good measure. Arkle simply possessed them all in superabundance.

As I wrote that sad Sunday when a newspaper rang me in sunshine and at my own happy stables with the news of his death, Arkle was a divine freak.

He was well-bred for his task, but not superbly so. His maternal side were prolific winner-producers in a limited class. His sire, though bred in the purple, was a racing flop. Arkle in his youth was far from being a paragon of equine beauty. He waddled. He was sold in the open market inexpensively. He was not, at first, highly considered by his wise old trainer, the late great Tom Dreaper. Dreaper, indeed, until Arkle was well into the middle of his Gold Cup treble, linked him with Prince Regent. And then Arkle went onwards, up and up.

How far would he have gone if his career had not been amputated in his prime? Dreaper, the man who would know, told me a few days before his death in 1975, that he believed Arkle would have gone on a long time for reasons given in the new additional chapters of this book.

There can be no follower of steeplechasing who would doubt that, at level weights, Arkle would have summarily disposed of the three winners of the three Gold Cups from 1967 to 1969 which followed the last of his treble. Woodland Venture, the winner in 1967 was, through his runner-up Stalbridge Colonist, at least two stone seven pounds inferior to Arkle. Fort Leney in 1968 was, as we have seen, assessed that year as three stone below Arkle. In 1969 Arkle was twelve. Even he could by then have been going over the hill. But the 1969 Gold Cup was won by another twelve year old, What a Myth, Arkle's contemporary, and at least three stone his inferior.

With no accident, with no leg troubles (and his *legs* were sound and firm till the day he died), with no coughs and colds (and he was a very healthy horse) what could possibly have prevented Arkle winning those three more Gold Cups to have given him a miraculous six in a row?

The extraordinary always fascinates. But the super-athlete, unless he has the spark of genius in him and the panache of the showman, can be dull. Arkle was the reverse. He had charisma, style, dash, character. He possessed, like Red Rum, those lovable things which made him not just a sportsman's hero, but the ordinary citizen's dream. He preferred, as his owner the Duchess of Westminster relates in this revised edition, the company of people to horses. This would explain his most unusual relationship with us. He gave to me a sensation of such extraordinary, penetrating understanding out of those eyes that his look still disturbs me nine years later.

He was exceptionally intelligent, as you will read, and this in itself is strange. Clever horses are often too bright to relish the ardours and buffets and strains of a very tough sport indeed. He had brilliance, but it was not flawed with its usual accompanying crack of instability. Of all the horses Arkle's old jockey Pat Taaffe has known, he puts Captain Christy the closest—'*If only he were right in the head.*' Arkle's mind had the perfect combination for a performer: total concentration of energy when required; total relaxation when not. Now this mental control can hardly be taught to humans, and never to horses. And though Arkle had the great fortune to spend his life always in kind and knowledgeable hands, even these could not have made his wonderful temperament.

Often, too, the horse who easily conquers will not struggle when adversity finally pummels him. Yet how Arkle struggled on his dire last day at Kempton, as the pain in his broken foot hurt more on every stride and even more as he jumped.

His swagger in the paddock, and the heights to which he often soared like an eagle surplus feet over the top of his fences, spring fresh in our hearts. And the way he would gaze, head up and slightly tilted, towards the heavens, staring at, listening to . . . what?

By one of those weird coincidences which often couple

greatness, the only other famous horse I know who gazed this way is the heroic Red Rum. And he is the only horse to match Arkle in vast popular appeal. Their stories are so very different. Their origins, up-bringing, early treatment could not have been less alike. I have written in *Red Rum* of the great differences between the lives of these two equine heroes, who tower above the ordinary horses in the light of public appeal: the Grand National horse who had it tough nearly all the way, and the Gold Cup aristocrat who enjoyed that loving kindness all his days which I have chronicled here to their very end.

They may be compared in stature. Their courage is equal. They shared another thing too: both will always be remembered and discussed. This is the full story of Arkle.

Ivor Herbert, Bradenham, 2003

One

THE HORSE Arkle was first thought of in 1956 in an old grey house built rather like a boat, but squatting 700 feet up a hill in the north of County Dublin.

The grim, grey farm buildings in two yards and the redoubtable barns – like fortresses – are older still, while Malahow House near Naul was built about two centuries ago by a Commodore Baker. The naval gentleman is a direct ancestor of the family which still lives there and farms 300 acres of damp and hilly land around it. The Commodore descended from the most famous Baker to arrive in Ireland – Colonel Henry Baker, who, with the Rector of Donaghmore, George Walker, was chosen to be Governor of Derry (or Londonderry as it was later called) during its great, unconquered siege in 1689.

Colonel Baker then was defending, until he died in the besieged city, a Protestant stronghold for 'King Billy' (William III) against the forces of the deposed James II, who had been booted out of Britain the previous year. The Baker family, though moving south so long ago into the predominantly Catholic part of Ireland, have remained Protestant throughout. After Derry their coat of arms became a gate and a key, and with them a goat, for Governor Baker, knowing that goats can live on very little, had had flocks driven into the city before he locked the gates.

It would not be surprising if there were now added to the Baker arms an intelligent horse, with large eyes and huge hooped ears, leaping over a host of Gold Cups, for the Bakers of Malahow would be the first to admit that it is nearly 300 years since equivalent fame lit upon their family.

For them, perhaps, it is fortunate that their house, screened by a thick platoon of black elms above an unsigned by-road, is not easy for a stranger to find. Though it now has electric light, and even a television set on which the activities of its most famous son are watched with 'oohs' and 'aahs' and clutching of strands of his shiny black tail, it has not yet been troubled by the telephone. 'I've been thinkin' about havin' it put in though,' says Mrs. Mary Baker, a sprightly widow with the boldness of a robin, who was a semi-invalid who kept to her room for nearly six years until Arkle started winning.

Mrs. Baker was born some sixty years ago only seven miles away from Malahow, but she speaks like an Edwardian English aristocrat, dropping her g's lightly as a parasol and without the brogue expected from an Irish farmer's wife and found in good measure on the tongue of her tall son, Harry.

Harry has charge of the 300 acres of old, permanent grass on limestone, which produces bullocks and sheep as well as mares, foals, hunters . . . and one wonder horse. The fields are large, varied and wet, and no better fenced than they need be. No artificial fertilisers are used so that no chemical companies can claim 'Our XYZ alone reared Arkle'.

Ireland has always grown good beef and great horses, and its farmers – through past poverty, keen instinct, or a dislike of changing anything before tomorrow – have kept the plough off their marvellous old grass, and the mixed goodness of centuries has been there for the cropping.

In England in wartime the ploughs tore through the grass-land, and the experts with seed to sell made virtue of necessity: 'Out with the old grass! In with the new magic mixtures! Slap on the artificial fertilisers!'

But the old herbs and the old grasses, with roots which go down and suck up the salts and minerals horses need, had gone with the plough. And English stud owners still wonder why their stock don't thrive, or are as fat and soft as Christmas turkeys!

The daily management of the Baker horses is conducted by

Harry's sisters, Alison and June, with some help from a farm man. Tommy Tiernan, who helped with Arkle and took him to the sales, is not there any longer, but is 'workin' on the buildin' '. The present help is, however, some relation, and there have been Tiernans with the Bakers for a very long time.

On matters of history such as the names of fields all defer to Mrs. Baker. 'This field by the road that Arkle was in when the hounds came by we called "The Queen Anne's" I think, but we'd better check with my mother.'

'It's called "The Grenans" ' said old Mrs. Baker crisply, 'after some people that lived there once years ago. You saw the old ruins down there?' I had when looking at Arkle's young nephew and niece in the field he had known.

'The Grenans' lies beyond the road at the foot of the hill from which Malahow stares out southwards. In it the young horse Arkle had spent most of his three years growing up. From it he had been led into the dark of his stable, up above the house when the hounds came past to set the young stock galloping. It's good hunting there with two packs: the Ward Union Staghounds and the Fingall Harriers. From it, on the rare clear day, you can see over the flat tangle of emerald fields and straggly fences and grey lanes to beyond the capital, to the Dublin Mountains.

When the soft wind's washed the wet from the sky you can see to Kildare, where Arkle's mother met his father, and to Greenogue, only five miles away as the fat rooks flap, where Arkle was to spend his life in training. And at night you clearly see the swivelling light of Collinstown Airport where Arkle was so often to stroll aboard a comfortable 'plane for a two hour hop to London airport and another victory in Britain.

Mrs. Baker was much younger than her husband – a very tall man, looking sternly out of a brown photograph under a wide brimmed trilby. She learned about horses from him, and passed it on to their children. 'He was always very keen about horses. He knew a lot. He could size 'em up at a glance, if you see what I mean, and he was very accurate.'

Mrs. Baker used to watch her husband considering what

stallions to pick for his mares. There have always been three or four brood mares on the place as long as anyone can remember, so that Malahow well illustrates those basic qualities of Irish breeding which so overwhelm the steeplechasing world: mares of the best jumping families, the produce reared on the best of old grass on good limestone land in a mild climate, tended by horse-lovers and given time.

There are no longer so many Bakers and Malahows over Ireland. The drift to the towns and the roar of the tractor has meant fewer men with enough wise time to care for horses. But offspring of the grand old steeplechasing families still abound if you know where to look, and they continue to dominate all jumping courses in the British Isles. All the best horses I bought and trained came from Ireland; only a couple of English-bred jumpers won us any races. Few are the great races in the National Hunt Calendar which aren't won year after year by Irish-bred horses. So long as this continues English jumping trainers will continue coming back with their cheque-books open, and it will be well worth the small Irish farmer keeping an old mare about the place. And the passage of the comet Arkle across the Irish jumping sky gave hope a blithe squeeze in the ribs again from County Monaghan down to County Cork.

They're not as expensive as the bleaters make out either, if you buy from the backwood farms and take your time. A good 'gas' and a drink are three parts of an Irish horse deal, but few rich English trainers have the time for either; their horses, bought from accessible smart stables, therefore cost a packet.

In a triangle round Malahow, 'with sides only a mile or two long,' as Mrs. Baker proudly points out, were bred or reared the Grand National winners Reynoldstown and Gregalach, and the Classic winners Santa Claus and Ballymoss. Golden Miller and Easter Hero were also bred on the Co. Meath and Co. Dublin border. Such a cluster of quality in so minute a plot of Ireland cannot be mere coincidence. But even with the boon of hindsight I can't say I would rush back to buy anything reasonable looking from the same magic triangle. Zero can't come up that often. Lightning's unlikely to strike again. This must have been the general opinion of the observant and informed in 1957 when Ballymoss was winning the English St. Leger just under five months after Arkle was born at the Ballymacoll stud, in Co. Meath, at 3.30 in the morning of April 19th, 1957.

A year earlier his dam, Bright Cherry, barren at the time, had visited Archive at the Loughtown stud in Co. Kildare, and had been successfully covered by him on May 2nd, 1956, when Arkle was conceived.

The choice of Archive, superbly bred by Nearco out of Book Law but a complete flop on the racecourse, had to be Mrs. Baker's own, for she was now a widow. Her choice, like her circumstances, was somewhat circumscribed. Her husband's death had meant the payment of quite heavy Death Duties, and Malahow, though as marvellously hospitable to unbidden, and unannounced and total strangers as are most Irish farms, does not have central-heating or close carpeting, or a large motor-car or smart garden. It is a working holding.

So it was to cheap stallions, those standing at under £50, that the Baker mares had to go. 'I just couldn't afford dear stallions, and that's plain English, though I'm Irish,' said Mrs. Baker, flinging her shawl around her, and snapping off a bit of biscuit with a grin and a twinkle, and a sniff of the nose.

In her husband's lifetime she had often read out the stallion advertisements in *The Irish Field* and suggested flat race sires. 'But my husband wouldn't hear of it. "They're *flat* horses", he'd say, don't y'know, and so we generally sent the mares to horses like Mustang.'

In fact, since she retired to stud in 1951, Bright Cherry had visited Mustang three times, having first a bay filly in 1952, then a chestnut filly in 1955 (of both of which more later) and being barren to him in 1956, the year she visited Archive.

Mrs. Baker declares loyally that her late husband had often talked about Archive for Bright Cherry and that it had always been his intention to send her to him. She adds, 'I looked up the horse's breedin' and saw it was good on the flat and I got an idea into my head: "introduce speed". It would give "pep".'

Archive is dead now. Bred by the second Viscount Astor in 1941, he went to stud in 1946 after a miserable wartime racing career in which he failed to win for two seasons. He was only three times third and once second in a poor race at Stockton. His lack of speed, which would have been disappointing in the son of a cheap stallion and an undistinguished mare, was in his case almost shocking: his sire Nearco was one of the greatest racehorses and sires in Europe since the war; his dam Book Law was in the opinion of top bloodstock expert John Hislop 'the best filly ever bred at Cliveden.'

The combination should, in the wishful theory of breeders, have yielded a classic winner. Book Law herself was second in the 1,000 Guineas and the Oaks and won the St. Leger. At stud she produced six winners, including the topclass mile-and-a-quarter horse, Rhodes Scholar, who in his turn sired the classic winner Black Tarquin.

But the bluest blood isn't worth catsmeat without ability and guts, and at the English 'Gaffs' of an Easter Monday you will see poor sad geldings bred to win a Derby but still banging round with groggy legs and sour eyes in the rear of selling hurdle races.

But ability can lie doggo in mares and stallions and sometimes get transmitted.

Those who now praise Arkle's 'class' – and he does indeed stand out like an 18th century Duke in Soho or Richard Burton in an undergraduate play – shouldn't wonder. His sire carried the blood which could have won him classics. Archive might have retired to stud in 1946 worth £200,000 and had his services sold for £1,000 a visit. But in that case of course Bright Cherry could not have afforded the pleasure.

Arkle's extended purple pedigree appears as a pull out in this book, drawn out as a labour of love by Captain Michael Hall, a talented Irish artist and manager of Goff's, the internationally famous bloodstock auctioneers who were to sell Arkle in August 1960. The pedigree shows that through Book Law, Arkle goes back to the Rosebery family's great tap-root mare Chelandry from whom descend the winners of ten classics!

Captain Hall had discovered one of these piquant coincidences which pepper the racing world: on both sides of his pedigree Arkle traces to Bend Or, the first Duke of Westminster's great racehorse who won the Derby in 1880. And in 1879 his grandson was born, christened Hugh Richard Arthur but always called 'Bendor' – the future second Duke of Westminster who, when 68 in 1947, was to marry as his fourth wife, Miss 'Nancy' Sullivan from County Cork, now Anne, Duchess of Westminster, owner of Arkle. The late Duke died, aged 74, in 1953, four years before Arkle was born.

Talking of Archive now, Mrs. Baker reflects that 'he'd been doin' pretty well at stud: Mariner's Log, and so on'. In 1955, when Mrs. Baker selected him for Bright Cherry, he'd had five winners of seven races on the flat at home and abroad, including the good sprinter Arcandy (here perhaps was evidence of the 'pep' Mrs. Baker was seeking), and five winners of $7\frac{1}{2}$ races under National Hunt Rules, including Gallerio and Lord Bicester's Mariner's Log, who at that stage was only promising.

Even Archive's stud performance was thus by the start of 1956 in no way exciting. Only by the end of that year when Bright Cherry was safely in foal to him, could the sharpest-eyed breeder deduce from the further victories of his offspring Gallerio, Mariner's Log, Help Yourself, High Gear, Rath Hill, Tom Oliver and Wrong Word (11 races worth £2,012 10s.) that Archive, like a number of well-bred but disappointing animals, seemed likely 'to turn out the odd decent jumper'.

Mrs. Baker's faith was in any case by no means founded in him. Indeed, she never sent Bright Cherry back to him again.

And this illustrates the greatest difficulty for the breeder of steeplechasing stock: it is likely to take six years from the time your mare is covered until you know if the five-year-old progeny is even headed for the top. In those six years stallions, mares, breeders and owners die, and most of the great Irish 'chasing sires become famous only posthumously.

Even if Mrs. Baker and Alison, June and Harry and all their friends and advisors had been convinced that Archive and Bright Cherry would prove the best steeplechasing mating of all time, it would have done them no good at all. For, until six years had passed, Bright Cherry declined to produce anything more at all.

As the young Bakers say – and no one could dispute it – she probably reckoned she'd produced such a horse that she needed six years rest. But it was not, of course, until 1962 that Arkle as a five-year-old began to unfurl the banners, and in that year Bright Cherry consented to breed again: to a stallion called Ballysway who ran out with his mares and served them 'nature's way'. The produce of this match was a chestnut colt foaled on April 27th, 1963 – a bold, hardy three-year-old when I saw him in the cold early spring of 1966. He was offered for sale, part broken and with a clean vet's certificate at Goff's sales on August 4th, 1966 but failed to reach his reserve. The racing world will be watching for his appearance.

Thus started on the right road again in 1962 old Bright Cherry aged twenty produced another chestnut colt in 1964 this time by Escart III, was barren in '65, had a colt by top sire Vulgan in 1966 at the age of twenty-two, and then visited Off Key. 'He's by Nearco, too, d'y'see?' said Mrs. Baker with a little bob and the ghost of a wink.

Bright Cherry looked only a teenager out in 'The Lawn' field on a February morning in 1966. She was queen of her lesser companions and found being photographed such a bore – ludicrous Englishman squatting down on the wet sedge grass and making Sassenach hunting cries – that she took sharp nips out of the youngster with her, and gave me the benefit of her shaggy backside. She is chestnut, smaller than I expected, and has a look of Arkle only in her ears. Probably, like Mrs. Baker, whose husband bred her, she reckoned the English visitor was asking too many tomfool questions.

Which leads us to her mother, the old brown mare Greenogue Princess, born in 1928, and died in 1951, twenty-three years old and the dam of a fleet of eleven winners. It was her early connection with trainer Tom Dreaper, plus her marvellous record at stud, which was to lead to her grandson Arkle's purchase in August 1960, by Anne, Duchess of Westminster and to Tom Dreaper's momentous even money second pick of him a year later.

Two

IN THE year 1940, when most of the rest of Europe was engaged in nearly winning, almost losing a world war, the Irish remained resolutely neutral – while sending their sons across in tens of thousands to fight for the Britain so many of them protest they detest. In that alarming summer the mare Greenogue Princess, then twelve years old, arrived at Malahow with some of her relations. In this way were the foundations laid for the advent of her grandson Arkle seventeen years later.

The mare only had to travel up the handful of miles from the farm close by Tom Dreaper's at Greenogue but the move caused argument then and reverberations still rumble lightly, I think, round the horizon's rim.

Wildly-generous would be the man who didn't regret that the means of producing Arkle (and more to come) had left his side of the family. Taking Arkle's average annual earnings at only £12,000, it would require a capital amount of £240,000 to yield this return annually at five per cent. And though Arkle's earnings are, unlike dividends, subject to his running expenses of about £1,500 a year, his winnings are free of tax, i.e. on British taxation levels – excluding surtax – they are worth two thirds as much again as taxed income.

Greenogue Princess had belonged to and was bred by Mrs. N. J. Kelly of Greenogue, who had been a widow for sometime. She had no children when she died in 1940, and so it was that instead of the broodmares and breeding stock remaining with the Kelly relations, they passed into the hands of her nearest relative. This was her younger brother whom we know as Mr.

Henry Baker of Malahow House, whose widow still survives him as we've seen.

When Mrs. Kelly was Miss Harriet Baker – but always called 'Dearix' – she was growing up with her brother Henry at Malahow in the last decades of the 19th century. She stayed at home, in fact, until she married N. J. Kelly as the last century slipped away, and went the six miles southwards to Greenogue to live with him on his substantial farm.

Mr. Nicholas Kelly, like nearly everyone then and now in that part of Ireland who is neither a pauper nor a cripple, was a very keen hunting man. To this end about the time of the Great War, he bought a mare called Cherry Branch II from Mr. Hugh Malcolmson, the father of the present Irish Turf Club Steward, Mr. George Malcolmson. He was probably keener on her performance in the hunting field (and the 'Wards' really race on after their carted deer) than on her breeding. But it was satisfactory that this Cerasus mare was out of Lady Peace, who was by General Peace, winner of the 'Lincoln' and a top class hurdler. So Mr. Kelly hunted Cherry Branch with the Ward Union Staghounds and afterwards ran her regularly at Fairyhouse and won the Ward Hunt Cup with her three times. She therefore turned out far better than an excellent hunter: she was a topclass hunter-'chaser.

When she retired she bred Cherry Tree (winner of two flat races, six hurdle races and three steeplechases), another winner Prince Cherry and, in 1928, Greenogue Princess.

Two years later in 1930, a sporting young farmer of thirty-two called Tom Dreaper – a quick, keen, thrusting hunting-man and a first-class performer in point-to-points – arrived in Kilsallaghan and settled into the farm in which he has lived and generally prospered ever since. He had been born – and so had his grandmother – at Donaghmore, a mile away, where his elder brother was still farming in the spring of 1966. With so many characters, horse and human, in this story sprouting from the one pocket handkerchief within an hour's ride of Greenogue Tom Dreaper's father is an exception: he had come originally from as far south as Kilkenny, nearly 100 miles away, a noticeable distance in Ireland even these days, when the country Irish call Dublin 'town' and make a thing of travelling in there and meeting up.

In the early 30's Tom Dreaper was essentially a farmer who loved his hunting and racing and just kept the odd horse. He started, as most farmer-trainers do, with one just 'outside' horse: one of the earliest horses he trained was one whose name even he has long forgotten but which belonged to Henry Baker. 'It wasn't much,' says Tom Dreaper, but it forged the first link between the families. So it was natural that Henry Baker's widowed sister Mrs. 'Dearix' Kelly a mile down the road, should ask Tom Dreaper to take her mare Greenogue Princess. 'She wasn't much good in training either,' Tom remembers, though she was placed under Rules and he himself won a race on her at the Fingall Harriers Point-to-Point.

Dreaper wasn't even confident about the point-to-point. 'I had a fellow stand by the second last fence to catch her when she fell and put me up again. Only for that she didn't fall!'

Even without having Arkle as a grandson old Greenogue Princess rates as an outstanding steeplechasing broodmare. Very few others exceed in total her twelve different winning offspring: My Richard, My Cherry*, Bay Branch, Gold Branch*, *Bright Cherry*, Prairie Prince, King's Inn, Greenflax (with whom I was to win a couple of races), Bomber Command, Knight of Greenogue*, Red Branch* and Lucca Prince. Four of these won on the flat, including My Cherry one of the four offspring marked * to whom Bright Cherry (Arkle's dam) was full sister.

These five were all by another topclass jumping sire, the speedy Knight of the Garter (a son of the great stayer and jumping sire, Son-In-Law). Most Knight of the Garter horses have proved fast, natural jumpers with a touch of the speed he'd needed to win at Ascot as a two-year-old.

Bright Cherry, it seemed certain, possessed the best sort of jumping breeding and it was reasonable to hope when Greenogue Princess gave birth to her in 1944, that she might prove almost as good as a broodmare as her mother, and a better performer on the course.

The sire of Greenogue Princess was My Prince, one of the greatest influences as a steeplechasing sire in the last thirty years, and a name still eagerly sought for as he recedes down and down the long corridors of jumping pedigrees. He sired those four superlative 'chasers Reynoldstown, Royal Mail, Gregalach, and Easter Hero and also the horse who was the greatest Tom Dreaper trained till Arkle came along: the late J. V. Rank's wonderful 'chaser, Prince Regent.

When Bright Cherry was born, her dam had been four years with the Bakers at Malahow. Mr. Henry Baker liked seeing his royal-blue-and-white-striped colours on the track, and he resolved to send the chestnut mare to Kilsallaghan, where her mother had come from, to be trained by Tom Dreaper.

Although Dreaper had been farming at Greenogue since 1930, he had trained only a handful of horses there (including a few of the Baker's) until 1938. In that year of the Munich Crisis someone else's tragedy started the forty-year-old Dreaper on his climb towards the summit as a racehorse trainer. That summer a young man called Paddy Power from Co. Waterford, who had charge of four of the great J. V. Rank's young 'chasers, was killed in a car accident on his way to the Dublin Horse Show. All four horses came to Tom Dreaper at Greenogue. One was Prince Regent.

Nothing so makes a trainer as a brilliant horse. A sound little man may win more than his fair share of little races at unnoted meetings year after year. Except for his satisfied patrons, no one will regard him as being anything better than a 'Third Division' fellow. At Cheltenham in 1955 a revered racing correspondent told me gravely that 'though Ryan Price could win small races, he hadn't enough class to train the winner of the Champion Hurdle.' Price's Clair Soleil won it that afternoon, and ever since I've doubted this sort of sweeping condemnation (to which observers of the racing scene are prone). Two years later in the paddock, before Linwell's Gold Cup win, I observed the same correspondent eyeing me with gloom, and I wondered how many times that day he had already dismissed me. He had in fact backed Linwell heavily!

Prince Regent was the first rocket which, even in wartime, signalled to the world that Dreaper was a first class trainer of first class horses. He won the horse's first race riding himself in a flatrace at Naas in 1940. The great horse, in the restricted racing of those years, went on to win eighteen more races including the Gold Cup of 1946 (strangely he was the first Irish horse to do so) and an Irish Grand National. There was no Grand National at Aintree from 1941 until 1946. In the latter year Prince Regent, aged eleven and humping 12 st. 5 lb. was 3rd to Lovely Cottage and Jack Finlay beaten only four lengths and three, one of the greatest-ever performances at Liverpool. It is not surprising that, even twenty years later, Dreaper hangs back from comparing Arkle with the legendary 'Prince'. What might that horse have won and done had he raced in peacetime? And how great is the debt each flourishing trainer owes to his first name-spinning hero?

The late J. V. Rank had other top horses in his powerful string at Greenogue, including Shagreen, Keep Faith and Red Branch, the last being Arkle's aunt – Bright Cherry's full sister. The late Lord Bicester had joined the stable too, with certainly the handsomest and often the best big Irish 'chasers of their year, like the brilliant Royal Approach (who in his first two seasons did as much as Arkle was to do in his, before he cracked a bone in his knee), Bluff King, and Mariner's Log. The last was the Archive horse whose success suggested to Mrs. Baker that his sire might prove a good mate for Bright Cherry.

The strings draw together. In 1946 a tall young amateur rider christened Patrick, son of Irish trainer Tom Taaffe, had his first ride under Rules when he rode Lord Bicester's young star Finnure in his first race in Ireland. Finnure was to hit the heights in England, winning Kempton's King George VI 'chase in 1949 and being second in Cottage Rake's third consecutive Gold Cup in 1950.

Pat Taaffe stayed in Ireland as an amateur, riding a string of winners on horses trained by his father, Tom Taaffe, at

Rathcoole, in which grey village on the Dublin-Naas road he was then living. Mr. P. Taaffe rode for a number of other owners and trainers too, and then at the end of 1949, Tom Dreaper's stable jockey, Eddie Newman, broke his knee in a fall in England. Dreaper asked Pat Taaffe to ride, still as an amateur, and his first two rides for the stable before Christmas at Leopardstown were both winners. He had been thinking of turning professional and then, early in 1950, the revered Tom Dreaper offered him the sparkling job of first stable jockey. Taaffe turned professional, as the Stewards had been suggesting he should do, and one of the best and most enduring post-war racing partnerships was sealed. Sixteen years later Pat Taaffe, with almost every jumping prize in his pocket, says simply, 'I owe *everything* to Mr. Dreaper.' His admiration is total.

To start with, Martin Molony was still riding J. V. Rank's horses and some of Lord Bicester's. Then when Martin retired, Pat Taaffe 'sort of took over, you know . . .' The horses he rode at Greenogue included such stars as Roimond, Greenogue, Shagreen, Early Mist, Royal Approach, Stormhead and the mare Bright Cherry, who ran her last race at Naas on May 12th, 1951, carrying topweight and Pat Taaffe into third place in a 2¼ mile 'chase. She was seven years old. Three weeks later she was at stud, was covered by Mustang on June 2nd and conceived the bay filly to be named Cherry Tang. Quick in all her races, Arkle's mother could hardly have made a quicker start to her stud career. Bright Cherry had had her first race as a four-year-old on July 31st, 1948 at Baldoyle, ridden by Dreaper's then stable jockey, Eddie Newman, and finished third of six to the odds-on winner Hill of Tara, beaten sixteen lengths in a two mile hurdle race.

Bright Cherry is on the small side and has been widely described as a complete non-stayer, barely able to last out two miles unless on road-hard ground with the wind behind her. In fact, she stayed 2½ miles when the ground was firm, she was an excellent jumper and, even by the high standards of Dreaper's stable, extremely fast. She ended her racing career at the top of the handicap, having won altogether one hurdle race and six steeplechases (three in the summer of 1950, including the valuable Easter Handicap Chase at Fairyhouse), and she was also placed eleven times, all in the ownership of Mr. Henry Baker. The mare owed nobody anything. She would have had a successful and happy career if she had produced nothing at all at stud.

What is surprising, and deeply disappointing for the Baker family is that having produced her first foal with such dexterity so soon after leaving the stage, she has had so few live foals since. After giving birth to Cherry Tang in 1952 she visited Limekiln on June 25th, got safely into foal, and then, unhappily slipped it at the end of March 1953 when she'd been pregnant nine months.

Bright Cherry was sent back to Limekiln in June, 1953, but proved barren. Next year there was thus no need to wait so long and she was covered by Mustang on April 28th to produce on May Day, 1955 a chestnut filly foal which Mrs. Baker called Cherry Bud and which most fortunately for her she still owns. For this mare is now as valuable a piece of capital equipment as any in the National Hunt breeding world.

For Cherry Bud is half-sister to Arkle and only two years older, and she has already had three foals. The first, thanks to Arkle, really hit the jackpot for the Baker family, who had never expected more than about £500 for anything they bred and sold, a sum which barely repays for a three-year-old the cost of its keep and its mother's and the price of the stud fee and the weekly bills from the stud.

But in 1962, soon after Arkle had hinted that he might prove a useful racehorse, his half-sister produced a bay colt by Ireland's king jumping sire, Vulgan. This offspring went off to Ballsbridge sales as an unbroken three-year-old in August, 1965, and was sold to the American General Mellon, a patron of Dreaper's, for the colossal price of 4,600 guineas. The Baker family, six months later, were still rolling about in laughing delight and slapping their knees at the very recollection of such a fortune. The horse, named Vulture, was reckoned by Dreaper early in 1966 'to need a lot of time – but he's a nice young horse. He's all *right*.' He was to prove this on his first run.

Very wisely the Bakers continued the Vulgan mating, and as a result Mrs. Baker now has at home turned out at Malahow a full-brother and a full-sister to Vulture, foaled in 1964 and 1965 respectively. The brother may well be sold as a three-year-old and make great money. The sister will probably serve to continue the blood line.

Bright Cherry, after producing Vulture's dam Cherry Bud in 1955, returned to Mustang, but was barren again.

It was thus that Mrs. Baker, humming and hawing over the stallion advertisements and recollecting her late husband's advice and being aided by suggestions from her children, decided that in the spring of 1956 Bright Cherry should travel to the Loughtown Stud, near Slane, in Co. Kildare to visit Archive. He was not in fact proving either a popular or a fertile stallion. In 1954 he'd covered only eighteen mares and produced only nine living foals. The average distance over which his progeny won just exceeded $1\frac{1}{2}$ miles, but he had only had three winners in '55 from seventeen runners on the flat, and only two jumping winners between July, '54, and June, '55. The auspices looked anything but bright. But Bright Cherry was successfully covered by him on May 2nd and came home again to Malahow for her year of waiting. It was soon plain she was in foal and by the winter it was time to decide which stallion she should visit next spring.

It was satisfactory in 1956 that Bright Cherry was safely in foal, but not particularly exciting. Her second foal, Cherry Bud, was an unproved yearling still at home, as was her first foal, Cherry Tang, the bay filly by Mustang – now a five-year-old mare who had done nothing. There was no sign so far in the five years that Bright Cherry had been at stud that either the quantity or quality of her offspring was going to make the Baker family fortunes.

Mrs. Baker decided to ring the changes again and selected Straight Deal, Miss Dorothy Paget's wartime Derby winner who had proved very disappointing as a sire of equally classy flat races (except for some useful stayers), but who was producing a large number of jumping winners. In these respects he reflects a side pattern of English classic results: two other Epsom Derby winners, April the Fifth before him and Airborne after, both got excellent jumpers after disappointing with the best mares from the Flat.

In 1957 Straight Deal was standing at his owner Miss Dorothy Paget's substantial stud, Ballymacoll, more than 300 excellent acres near Dunboyne just inside the eastern boundary of Co. Meath and so quite close to the Bakers at Malahow and the Dreapers at Kilsallaghan.

So on March 29th, 1957, Bright Cherry, heavily in foal to Archive, climbed up into the C.I.E. horse box at Malahow House and bumped off down the plunging dark drive with the elm boughs swishing on its roof top for the thirty mile run south-west to Ballymacoll.

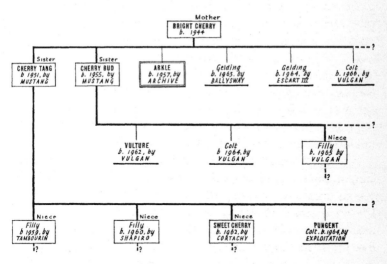

Family tree of Arkle's female relations. (see pages 37 and 38)

33

Three

TELEGRAM RECEIVED April 19th, 1957.
MISS BAKER, MALAHOW, NAUL. BRIGHT CHERRY
FOALED BAY COLT 3.30 AM THIS MORNING BOTH
WELL CHARLIE.

Charlie Rogers managed Ballymacoll for The Hon. Dorothy
Paget until her death in 1960. She had owned it for fifteen
years since buying it from the executors of old 'Boss' Croker.
Miss Paget, an eccentric, large supporter of National Hunt
racing, never went near the place, though she bred good
winners there in Straight Deal (The Derby) and Nucleus
(Jockey Club Stakes). When she died, her executors sold it with
all her bloodstock in a package deal said to be around £250,000
to Mr. Michael Sobell, the television manufacturer who had
then had two good horses in training in England: London Cry,
the Cambridgeshire winner, with Sir Gordon Richards, and
Flame Gun, the top two mile 'chaser, with me. In February,
1966, old Flame Gun, pensioned off and with a young lady
friend was enjoying life and 14 lb. of oats daily in one of the
excellent paddocks at Ballymacoll.

Charlie Rogers is still in charge at Ballymacoll and Danny
Daly, who used to ride at Epsom for the late Tom Walls (the
actor and owner of April the Fifth) is still the Stud Groom who
was in at Arkle's birth. Still there too is Jimmy McEnery, from
Limerick the 'night man' who stayed up in his little room
between the two large foaling boxes when Bright Cherry
started her labours and who was first to see Arkle appear.

What the newly-born bay colt first saw under the bright

electric lights that April night was one of Ballymacoll's two huge foaling boxes (see picture between pp. 24 and 25), three times larger than an ordinary loose box, with deep straw frisked up two feet high all round. Jimmy McEnery had been watching through the panel in the door to his night-room and had sent round the word to Danny Daly.

The birth was easy and completely forgettable, though the date sticks in the minds of his connections: by one of these strange coincidences Arkle's birthday is sandwiched exactly by that of his future owner, Anne, Duchess of Westminster on April 18th, and that of the young woman who brought him up, Alison Baker, on April 20th. Nine years later Charlie Rogers didn't think Arkle had been born at Ballymacoll at all – 'I'm sure he wasn't.' Daly scratched his head: 'Was his dam the chestnut one or the brown mare?'

The chestnut, Bright Cherry, and her colt foal stayed at the stud for two months, but there were thirty-two other mares visiting Straight Deal that spring and summer. At public studs where a stallion stands the rapid turnover of mares and foals each covering season prevents many sticking in the minds of the staff, unless the mare is particularly famous or unless she or her foal get into trouble. Bright Cherry then was not important outside her family, and her foal fortunately survived any disaster.

A few days after being born he and his mother were moved a hundred yards from the foaling boxes (needed for other visiting matrons) to a neat range of eight others diagonally across a grassy courtyard. Here they joined other mares and foals and were led out each day past the gaunt, empty house on its little knoll, and down the sweeping avenue of huge mixed trees, and then turned right into a level paddock, large as two football grounds.

Here Arkle tottered, then trotted, then cantered about as summer came in and the leaves thickened and the grass came spurting through. And Bright Cherry vainly visited Straight Deal. They could hardly have stayed longer, and nearly every other mare and foal had left Ballymacoll by June 28th, when the barren Bright Cherry and Arkle set off for Malahow.

It was at this point that Arkle had his first accident. Either climbing up into the horsebox to come home, or on the way back, he gave himself a nasty bang on a hindleg just above the hoof. The little foal wasn't lame when he got out of the C.I.E. box for his first look at Malahow, but the injury was serious enough for Mr. 'Maxie' Cosgrove, the renowned and sporting veterinary surgeon who looked after the Baker horses to come over and have a look. He recollects the enlargement (its trace remains nine years later) and took an X-ray. There was no permanent damage to the bone beneath, and the first anxiety was over, but it had been a close shave. Cosgrove 'wasn't very impressed with the foal. He was a hardy little lad, that's the best you could say.'

Alison Baker recollects thinking him merely 'a decent looking foal.' He was brought out of his box in the Lower Yard and round to the front of the house, so that Mrs. Baker, then very much the invalid, could have a peep down at him out of her bedroom window.

The Bakers thought 'he wasn't so much gangling, as scopey,' and they reckoned that he would need a lot of time to develop. So it was resolved since they couldn't afford to keep him in training themselves, that he would go off to Goff's Sales at Ballsbridge, Dublin, as a three-year-old.

There's no pampering of the horses at Malahow. The day after Arkle arrived he was turned out with his mother in The Pond Field, a flat plateau just off the upper yard. For the first two or three weeks he and Bright Cherry were brought in together every night, and turned out each morning. After that they were turned out altogether in the field called The Lawn (see picture between pp. 24 and 25) on the other side of the farm, where I saw old Bright Cherry, in foal again, grazing, nine years later.

It was now August. Since no one thought Arkle very special and there were a lot of horses on the place, it had been decided to send his eldest sister, the five-year-old bay mare, Cherry Tang, by Mustang, off to the Ballsbridge Sales. Had the Bakers the gift of second sight, and could envisage that the recently-arrived little colt foal was likely to prove even moderately successful on the racecourse, the mare Cherry Tang would have stayed right there at Malahow, awaiting the day when the deeds of her young brother would make her a highly valuable brood mare.

But she came up for sale on August 8th, 1957, and neither her looks nor her breeding encouraged the bidders to fall over each other in the open market. It was left to an Englishman, a Mr. T. Sanger, to buy her in his wife's name for the 'hunter' price of 380 guineas.

It turned out that Mr. Sanger had a permit to train his own horses and didn't want to waste time. Only ten weeks later the mare appeared on an English racecourse. Between October 26th and November 23rd Cherry Tang's new owner-trainer ran her three times in £140 novice hurdle races at Chepstow, Warwick and Worcester, ridden each time by J. Birch and always a rank outsider. In her first race she was tailed off and had to be pulled up. In her last two races she trailed round 'also ran but made no show.' She was not a harbinger of family fortunes.

Arkle's sister's racing record was short, useless and forlorn. The thought keeps nudging through: would she have made a racehorse, given time? Did she, like her brother and so many Irish horses, require that thing of which so many English owners are short: time to let horses develop? Ten weeks after the sale Cherry Tang was running in a race. It was nearly sixteen *months* after Arkle was sold before he went racing. But Mr. Sanger took a quick view: after four weeks Cherry Tang's racing career was over and it was off to the stallion with her. At stud she did infinitely better, producing for Mr. Sanger four foals in her first six years:

  1959 chestnut filly by Cortachy
  1960 bay filly by Shapiro
  1962 Sweet Cherry, chestnut filly by Cortachy
  1964 Pungent, brown colt by Exploitation.

After which Anne, Duchess of Westminster, acted with her

admirable acumen. In 1959, when my Flame Gun beat her fancied Cashel View for Cheltenham's Cotswold 'Chase, she set about buying all my horse's younger relations. Now she tracked Mr. Sanger down and bought from him her great horse's eldest sister. The price will have been the devil of a lot more than the miserable 380 guineas the Bakers got for her that August day at Goff's in 1957, but the Duchess now owns one of Arkle's only two half-sisters.

It is interesting to see from the family tree on page 33 that Arkle's other female relations are already surprisingly numerous: the chances of the famous dynasty continuing are thus much higher than from the usual Irish family of few fillies and numerous non-productive geldings. Mr. Sanger is likely to have done wisely. At least by cutting short Cherry Tang's racing career so soon after it had tried to start, he got three fillies out of her before Arkle had won his first Gold Cup. And every filly has a chance of breeding something – Oh, not *as* good, but very near it!

The Bakers in August, 1957, weren't at all pleased with the price they'd got for Cherry Tang, but at least they hadn't got to keep her and feed her through another winter.

In October it was time for Bright Cherry's colt foal to be weaned. Arkle was taken away from his mother with the usual amount of bellowing and shouting, and spent the winter with the other young stock in the Pond Field, by the side of the Top Yard. As well as the pond it has a nice stone rubbing post in its centre, smoothed by the luxuriant rubbing of legions of tickly coats.

Here Arkle ran out with old Brandy, a veteran retired hunter, famous with the 'Wards', on whose broad back dogs would sit smiling for their photographs. His job now was in Alison's words, 'to be nursemaid and to mind the foals.'

Arkle started his primary education. He was being brought in every night to the stable in the Bottom Yard and this meant a little headcollar on him and a cavesson. With this Alison occasionally gave him what the Irish call 'a little ringing' (which we call lunging) in order to – as Alison says – 'get a bend on his neck.'

He was fed night and morning with oats very well rolled to which a mineral supplement called 'Rosette' was added. All this was normal procedure at Malahow. The foals ate much less each morning, because they were banging about in their boxes longing to get out into the wet yellow field again, where they could nip each others' necks and buttocks, stand on their hindlegs to spar like statues, and trot around stiff-legged, short tail up like a plume, laughing, which is how horses show their sense of humour. Two nights a week they had bran mashes mixed with codliver oil and enough oats to 'give them a decent taste.'

Alison Baker fed by hand and judged by eye: 'if an animal isn't doing well, I give him more. If he leaves, I cut down.'

January came and the foal became a yearling. In April the new grass was bright and sweet through the Pond Field, and the colt and his companions were out all the time and getting no feeds at all. Then, on April 20th Arkle nearly cut a leg off!

On that morning, a Sunday, two young fillies escaped from the Bottom Field below and made their way giggling, nickering and pushing about in the manner of girls relishing being on the loose, up to the hilltop behind the crest of the Pond Field. The fillies did their fair share of calling the boys out, and the next thing was that old Brandy, who should have known better, and young Arkle, who didn't regard a fence as a grave impediment with friends the other side, jumped out to join them.

That is, Brandy did, but he was experienced enough to look for trouble. He saw the strand of barbed wire running through the tangle of blackthorn and gorse on top of the bank. He jumped clear. Arkle didn't. The barbed wire caught him and, as he struggled, gripped him, and ripped into his small foreleg and tore the skin and flesh off in a great gaping flap a foot long down his off-fore cannon-bone.

'Maxie' Cosgrove was sent for and came speeding out. He cleaned the wound and dressed it and got the hanging flap fixed back in place again with forty stitches. Cosgrove gave him an anti-tetanus injection. 'Tough little colt' he remembers, 'but always rather a difficult horse to do anything to. He was never mean, mind you. He'd struggle all right, but he'd never bash you.'

'The wound healed in a week or so', Alison Baker remembers, but the scar will blemish the black shine of Arkle's off-fore until he dies.

It was May before the colt could be turned out again night and day, and the summer rolled, fat, warm and flyblown into August, and it was time to turn the colt into a gelding, as is the universal practice with keepers of jumping 'stores'.

Accepting the predominance of geldings in National Hunt racing as we do, it comes as a shock to find how many of Arkle's myriad, non-racing admirers imagine that he, like a Derby winner – or even the humblest three-year-old colt on the Flat – can retire to stud when racing's done and start begetting.

When they learn he was 'cut' as a yearling they wince, and complain, 'What a waste!' But the fact is, of course, that it would have been 500 to 1 against Arkle winning even one small steeplechase as a full horse.

About 5,000 jumpers are in training each season. They average about three years in the game, so that in the twenty-one years since peace came creeping out we've probably seen about 35,000 different jumpers on English tracks. There has only been one absolutely top class entire horse from all those runners in that time: Fortina, the French-bred six-year-old, who won the 1947 Gold Cup*.

In those twenty-one years only a handful of other entire horses have won over *fences* at all. Numerous colts have won over hurdles at the ages of three and four and sometimes a little older. Age is the first influence which turns the entire horse against jumping obstacles. After four, if he is normally sexed, he will be thinking about fillies. He becomes like a sultan, increasingly fastidious about the roughness and toughness of the jumping game in wintry weather. He starts to turn it in, particularly if asked to loft his fully developed body over big, thick painful steeplechase fences.

* Largely prepared by Charlie Mallon, then Hector Christie's Head Lad and later mine when he won another Gold Cup – but with his name in the records this time – ten years later, a few weeks before Arkle was born.

And the horse who 'will not', be he the most beautiful, swiftest animal since Genghis Khan swept out of the Orient, is not worth toffee-paper.

You therefore decide to have your 'chasing-bred yearling gelded, and the quicker this is done the better. The longer the wait the more chance of the young horse developing masculine traits: wilfulness, a thick neck, and an eye for the dames. Probably the most difficult type of horse to train is the gelding who was 'cut' too late: neither one thing nor the other, and subconsciously disturbed. The longer the delay, too, the more chance of castration setting them back physically: the older the horse the bigger the operation. Delay also means that even yearling colts can get into trouble with fillies in fields, as Arkle did.

The best time for gelding is the early autumn of their yearling days: after the flies have gone, before the frosts. In the circumstances it is no flannel to say the operation is quite painless and as quick as having two teeth out. Done in a jiffy with a local anaesthetic, the horse is out again in the fields and grazing again immediately after, unaware of what he's missing.

One last point: this doesn't *ever* justify the horse being called 'it'. Nothing so pains the horse-lover or placards your ignorance as saying 'it' about a horse. Horses are heroes and horrors, but always, *always* he – unless they're she.

Despite Arkle's bid for freedom when he wanted to join the fillies and nearly joined his ancestors, the Bakers don't recall that he was particularly oversexed as a yearling colt. And the perfection of his temperament now: pride without impertinence, assurance without swagger, fire plus resolution, wouldn't have continued had he remained an entire.

So Arkle was gelded when the autumn of 1958 rustled in, and from then on he ran out day and night, except when the hounds came crying over the hills and the horsemen sparked up the grey lane in that syrupy steam that hangs over hot hunters. When either 'The Wards' or the Harriers were due around, Arkle and his companions were led up from 'The Grenans' and hidden out of harm's way in the Top Yard stables.

He ran out all winter through until he was three months a two-year-old and March came whistling across the low fields and beat the elms black branches about and slammed the swinging doors of barns. As Alison Baker started to get on with his breaking, the triumvirate to which five years later he was going to bring world fame, was having a runner on the first day of Cheltenham's National Hunt Meeting. Anne, Duchess of Westminster's Cashel View ridden by Pat Taaffe and trained by Tom Dreaper, started favourite for the Cotswold Chase, but was beaten by Flame Gun. The Duchess, however, was now determined to go in for steeplechasing in a big way. She had owned at least one good horse before: old Sentina with Tom Dreaper, winner of eight races, including the National Hunt Handicap Chase at Cheltenham which he won twice, ran his last race at the age of eleven in October 1961.

Like most of the country Irish, the Duchess has as natural a love for horses as the urban Briton has for his 'telly'. Like him, too, she has a good eye for her favourite subject. She'd hunted regularly and well in her youth as Miss 'Nancy' Sullivan in Co. Cork. She was now the childless widow of one of Britain's richest men. First love, then time and money for the sport have made her steeplechasing's most successful owner ever. And, in spite of her advantages and victories, she has enough nice naturalness to remain most popular in a jealous age and a whips-out sport.

Alison Baker says that Arkle 'doesn't stand out as being bad' when she was breaking him – 'he wasn't troublesome at all.' But though he had, as we know, been lunged round in a cavesson as a foal, that was two years ago and Alison found that he wasn't as amenable as he had been.

She first started by 'handling him a bit' in the stable, rubbing him down, talking to him, then getting him used to the cavesson again. It was time for the breaking bridle and this she popped into his mouth for half an hour a day. Alison remarks, with pride in an expert's approbation, 'Mrs. Dreaper says *all* the horses from here are pretty well broken.'

After a few days of this Arkle had the tack put on him in the stable, and Alison led him round and round inside to get him used to the tickle and grip round his girth and the light weight squeaking on his back. Now she put the side reins on him, and had him out in the Yard with the long reins either side of him. 'This time there were fireworks all right!' But after bucking and kicking he settled down and Alison began to drive him ahead of her in long reins, so that he could feel the reins against his flanks and second thighs and hear her voice behind, encouraging him to go forward unled.

There is no better way of developing that *controlled boldness* which good racehorses, like good soldiers, like captains of industry or actors or any other leaders must possess. Few are the flat race youngsters who are given the time and taught their manners this way. Flocks of giddy yearlings are roughly broken in a few days and ridden away by hamfisted dwarf baboons hanging onto their mouths and drumming tiny heels into their startled sides. The result is a thousand flat race recruits each spring with no mouths, no steering, no brakes, no balance and no courage beyond that of following the dithering backside of the sheep in front. Their potential is minimised, their character repressed, and the only good thing about a shoddy, botched business is that few of the owners who've shelled out £3,000 or £13,000 for them a few weeks back have any notion of their ruin.

Fortunately for Arkle, and for Tom Dreaper, the Duchess, and all who rode him, Alison Baker did the job properly. She never backs the youngsters, preferring, with discretion, to leave that final stage, to the stable which buys the Malahow youngsters.

So by the end of May, 1959, Arkle's first lessons were done. He was turned out again day and night, but well fed in the fields during the ensuing winter until he became a three-year-old and was ready to be prepared for the Sales.

Looking back on those last days at Malahow Mrs. Baker remembers in tranquillity 'a good looking horse, but he kept his head high.' She was in bed most of the time. 'I wasn't very well for two years. So when I saw him it was always through a

43

window, looking down on him.' Mrs. Baker can't say how he moved in those days. 'I never saw him in the field, actually.'

I asked Alison Baker why she thought Arkle turned out to be such an exceptional horse. 'Because he's very intelligent. And he's a "kind" horse – things don't upset him too much – and he's an easy horse for people to get on with.' I wondered if he'd been intelligent as a youngster. 'He wasn't a dope, anyway, I can say that for him! He was an easy horse to break. Once he got it into his head that he was meant to do a thing in a particular way, he'd do it *always*, though it may have taken him a while to learn it. He was never vicious. No, never vicious at all. Just gay. Gay in himself, as he is today – gay!'

Four

IT HAD always been the Baker's intention to sell Arkle at Goff's Sales in August, 1960, though Tom Dreaper is sure that, if old Mr. Henry Baker had been alive he would have contrived to keep him in training himself.

The August Sales at Ballsbridge, which coincide with the best and strangest of all Horse Shows enjoying itself beyond the road, are far from being the classiest sales organised by Goffs. The highest quality yearlings come up in September. August, normally, is for the lesser mortals, and it would have occurred to no one, picking their way out to the pleasant, airy suburb of Ballsbridge from hotel, lodging house or noble house-party, that any real star could be found in the August Sales. Bargains certainly, particularly in the pale mornings when the last of the drunks weave home from the Hunt Ball in the City. But nothing of quality . . .

On the first day, Wednesday, August 3rd, 1960, a number of yearlings, largely bred for jumping, were disposed of through the spick, span and friendly sales paddocks for fairly modest prices. The highest price was 700 guineas and the Bakers noted with delight that this was paid for a yearling colt by Archive. This gave them great encouragement for the morrow.

The choice of Archive seemed to be paying off on the race-course, too. That summer he had had the winners of nine races worth £7,621 10s. on the Flat, including the handsome Ascot winner Farrney Fox, then a five-year-old. Under National Hunt rules in 1960 Archive was doing even better with twelve

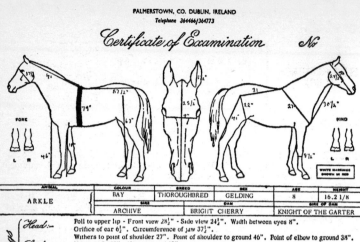

ANIMAL	COLOUR	BREED		SEX	AGE	HEIGHT
ARKLE	BAY	THOROUGHBRED		GELDING	8	16.2 1/8
	SIRE		DAM		SIRE OF DAM	
	ARCHIVE		BRIGHT CHERRY		KNIGHT OF THE GARTER	

Markings

Head:—

Limbs:—

Body:—

Augment:—

Remarks:—

Poll to upper lip - Front view 28½" - Side view 24½". Width between eyes 8".
Orifice of ear 6½". Circumference of jaw 37½".
Withers to point of shoulder 27". Point of shoulder to ground 46". Point of elbow to ground 38".
Hip to stifle 22". Hip to ground 63".
HIP TO HOCK: 41"
BONE: 8½". (Circumference below knee).
HEIGHT: 16.2 1/8 (shod).
GIRTH: 79"
Rein neck extended:- From poll to highest point of withers 41".
Withers to root of tail following contour of spine 51½".
Angle of jaw to point of shoulder 30½".
Withers to hip (external angle of ileum) 31".

Date.—   23rd December, 1965.   Measurements taken five days prior to winning King George VI Chase, Kempton.

S. M. Cosgrove, M.R.C.V.S.

Arkle's vital statistics in 1965

winners of twenty-one races, the biggest being Sea Wife a good mare I was training.

Surely, the Bakers thought on Wednesday evening, our Archive three-year-old will sell well tomorrow. He had been in the stables a month getting prepared. Maxie Cosgrove, one of the top six horse practitioners in the British Isles, had been out to worm him. 'He didn't like the stomach tube at all and he fought hard against it. He's always been like that at first – resenting something new being done to him until he knows what it's all about. Then he accepts it and becomes amenable.'

Cosgrove remembers particularly the excellence of his feet, and six years later declares 'A very sound horse. I've never met a sounder horse in training.'

Arkle was examined for his certificate of soundness. He passed easily, and it accompanied him to the sale to be lodged

Lot 148.

BAY GELDING
(1957)

		Nearco	Pharos
Archive 1			Nogara
(B. 1941)		Book Law	Buchan
			Popingaol
		Knight of the	Son-in-Law
Bright Cherry 41		Garter	Castelline
(Ch. 1944)		Greenogue	My Prince
		Princess	Cherry Branch II

This gelding has just been broken and driven in long reins, but not ridden.
16 hands. V.S. Certificate at Sale.

BRIGHT CHERRY, winner of a hurdle race and six 'chases, also placed
eleven times. Own sister to My Cherry, Red Branch, Knight of Greenogue
and Gold Branch. Above is her third produce.
GREENOGUE PRINCESS, dam of the winners **My Richard, My Cherry**
(dam of the winner Wild Cherry), **Bay Branch, Gold Branch, Bright
Cherry, Prairie Prince, King's Inn, Greenflax, Bomber Command, Knight
of Greenogue** and **Red Branch.**
CHERRY BRANCH II, winner of steeplechases, including Ward Hunt Cup
three times ; dam of **Cherry Tree** (winner of a flat race, a N.H. flat race,
six hurdle races and three steeplechases), **Prince Cherry** (winner) and
Greenogue Princess (see above).

Stabled in Box 148.
Lot 148 in the sale catalogue in 1960

in the auctioneers' long office behind the rostrum in the sale
ring. Here anyone interested in a Lot can ask to see his
certificate, noting not only what it says, but who said it. Some
veterinary surgeons are much tougher in their examination
than others. Some deservedly have a higher reputation for
knowledge and insight and judgement, all of which are vital in
the examination of unraced, unridden stock.

When the excellently produced catalogue came out the
Bakers had been pleased to find Arkle well placed: Lot 148,
about one third through Thursday, August 4th. Nobody ever
wants their horses to come up early in the morning: bidders are
few then, and 'cold', waiting to measure price-levels, hanging
back till they see what such-and-such makes, telling themselves
'there's plenty more to come.' For the cool, courageous buyer
the early lots offer bargains, but the auctioneers, aware of this,
place their inferior stock at the start of catalogues. And wise
men, knowing this, have another reason to hold back . . .

In those days the firm of Robert J. Goff was really showing
the way to Tattersall's, their antique English competitors in the
selling of bloodstock by auction. Goff's Ballsbridge premises

were bright and neat and rationally laid out. Tattersall's stabling at Newmarket was dark, tatty, and crazily disposed. Goff's produced lively catalogues; Tattersall's were less efficient. Goff's gave a warm welcome to sellers and buyers; Tattersall's appeared to think both were a bit of a nuisance. Tattersall's used to be rather reactionary – the basic failing which has so nearly ruined both British Flat-racing and (possibly) the Tory party. Fortunately for Tattersall's they shook off smug slumber in the nick. Worried by Goff's mounting share of the market they at last began to improve themselves and move with the times. They are modernised now and alert and polite.

The Bakers reckoned that Tom Dreaper would show some interest in their rather gangly three-year-old if only because of the racing successes of Bright Cherry, the breeding successes of Greenogue Princess and the general excellence of the family. They don't recall Tom Dreaper looking at Arkle at Malahow, though, unless it was when he was only a foal. Tom on the other hand thinks he went over to look at the horse a couple of times.

Be that either way, when he saw the Duchess over the road in the Royal Dublin Society's show Tom Dreaper merely suggested to her that she have a look at Lot 148 coming up on Thursday morning. He reminded her that he'd trained the dam who had a lot of speed, and that the family had produced a lot of winners. 'I don't say he'll stay more than two miles though', he warned.

Over in the show grounds, round those lovely little treelined rings where debs mix with tinkers, ambassadors jostle grooms and ponies' heads push past silk parasols, and the sweat of a hunter rubs off on a Paris coat, the Duchess had marked down a lovely young horse. This was also a three-year-old, but a magnificent looking individual (which Arkle was not) called Bray Flame, bred for chasing by Flamenco out of Brown Garter who – like Arkle's dam – was by Knight of the Garter. This three-year-old, owned by James McCabe of Downpatrick, Co. Down in Ulster, was being shown in the Hunters-in-Hand class, prior to going up for sale over the road.

The judges agreed that Bray Flame looked magnificent: he

won not only his class but the Pembroke Challenge Cup for the best young horse bred in Ireland suitable to make a hunter. The Duchess decided to buy him. She noted what Tom Dreaper said about the other three-year-old; they parted, and she went across to have a look at Lot 148.

The Duchess now teases Tom Dreaper by saying that he must also have recommended Arkle to a well-known judge of steeple-chasers, Captain Charles Radclyffe, who was also the step-father of the once leading amateur rider, Sir William Pigott-Brown, Bart.

Tom Dreaper probably did mention the horse to Radclyffe, who anyway looked at him, liked him and bid for him.

Tommy Tiernan had travelled the three-year-old to the sales, had installed him in Box 148 and stood by him to show him off to prospective bidders. A number of interested callers looked him over, felt his legs, queried the scar on his cannon-bone, spotted the lump on his hind coronet, opened his mouth and looked at his teeth, and asked Tommy Tiernan to trot him out on the grass between the lines of boxes so that they could watch his action. He didn't move particularly well, his frame was rather angular and everything about him suggested that, if he were ever to become anything, he would need expensive time to get there.

It was the Bakers' intention that he should be sold, and so his reserve price was kept realistically low. 'We didn't want him back,' says Alison Baker. Taking all factors into consideration they put on him a reserve of 500 guineas.

The morning's sales got slowly under way. Only seventeen horses had been sold by the time Tommy Tiernan led Arkle through the narrow 'throat' between the outer ring and the sales ring. Alison Baker, all of a twitter, was up in the auctioneer's rostrum. Only seventeen lots sold so far, several at under 100 guineas; the highest price – that for another three-year-old – was only 450 gns . . . The lot just going out, 'Trebor' a ten-year-old, had made only 140 gns. Surely their three-year-old would be lucky to reach his reserve . . .

As he entered the ring and Tommy began the slow circling

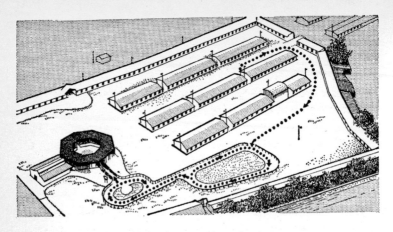

Arkle's route to the sale ring

which would continue till the hammer slapped the desk, the auctioneer began to recite his breeding: '. . . and a really well bred three-year-old here, gentlemen . . . His dam Bright Cherry . . . And a clean sound certificate . . . What may I ask you to start me: a thousand guineas? No? Eight hundred then? *Five* hundred? Come *on*, gentlemen, please . . .'

The bidding at last began. In a few exchanges it had reached and passed the reserve price and Alison was delighted. The bidding continued, two or three bidders still active. Each bid capping the other was however, genuine, as Alison knew: with the reserve price passed the auctioneer could make no bids himself. She could hardly contain herself as the price reached 1,000 guineas and still went on: 'One thousand and fifty then, thank you . . . And eleven hundred. Eleven hundred.' The auctioneer looked across at the previous bidder and raised an eyebrow. 'Thank you. Eleven hundred and fifty guineas, I'm bid . . . Any more at eleven hundred and fifty . . .? anymore . . .? I'm selling him . . . for the last time then . . . at eleven hundred and fifty guineas . . . SOLD.' His hammer cracked down. Tommy led the three-year-old out and back to his box. Alison darted down the back steps of the auctioneer's rostrum. Who had paid this huge price, the largest the Bakers had ever received?

Alison saw Tom Dreaper and asked him who'd bought the horse. 'The Duchess of Westminster,' he told her. The Irish Press came round to his box and took photographs of the gelding, for his was the highest price of the sales so far and Duchesses are news even if they only have graceful influenza.

Alison grabbed some hairs of his tail for luck, brought them home to her invalid mother, and Mrs. Baker has kept them ever since. Each time Arkle runs the now sprightly old lady grips the hairs in the palm of her hand as she watches on television and squeezes them tightly, for until February, 1966, at Leopardstown, she had never seen Arkle run in the flesh.

But the Duchess was not yet done. Six more lots were sold after her first purchase and all bar one under 700 gns., and then the show ring winner Bray Flame came up and she started bidding again. She had to go to 2,000 gns. to buy him. To put these prices into the perspective of flat racing it's worth noting that the highest price for a yearling of 1960 was 16,000 gns. paid by the Anglo-Irish Agency for Changing Times! (Archive's yearlings averaged a mere 483 gns.)

The Duchess's purchases certainly weren't cheap by the jumping price levels of 1960 and only one other horse in the whole catalogue cost more than Bray Flame. It's possible even six years later to buy good-looking well-bred three-year-olds unbroken for around £1,500 off Irish farms, but not, of course, from established training stables. Close relationship to a high class 'chaser could almost double the price.

1,150 guineas for Arkle's breeding and his looks was a very fair price. The Bakers were absolutely delighted with it, and really nobody that summer afternoon at Ballsbridge thought the purchase was likely to prove anything very special.

Two nice three-year-olds then were the Duchess's on the August 4th: the first with a lot of winners in his pedigree, the second with none, but much better looking. One of them when the time came a year later would go to Tom Dreaper; the other would go to the Duchess's other Irish trainer, the gay sprightly Willie O'Grady of Killeens, Ballynonty, down south in Tipperary.

O'Grady, forty-eight in 1960 when the Duchess bought Arkle and Bray Flame, had been top jockey in Ireland three times since he turned pro. in 1930. He had been training with success since 1940. Neither he nor Tom Dreaper, fourteen years his senior, knew that August day at Ballsbridge in 1960 which, if either, of the Duchess's two new three-year-olds they would get to train.

Anne, Duchess of Westminster, as we've already seen, is knowledgeable about racing and thorough in its pursuit. It was her sound practice then, as now, to send all new unbroken horses to her Cheshire home, Eaton Lodge, near Eccleston, Cheshire, on one of the famous Westminster estates. Here they are given part two of their gradual education, by being carefully broken in, backed, nagged and advanced by Mr. William Veal (brother-in-law of Colonel George Wigg, the Paymaster General and brother of two former professional jockeys) to the stage when they can immediately be cantered on reaching their trainers a year later.

Time is given to learn gradually the right way of moving, steering, stopping. Time is given to develop stature and strength and to become 'amiable', as Mrs. Betty Dreaper puts it. Of the time the three-year-old Arkle spent in Bill Veal's hands at Eaton Lodge, very few hours were wasted for this is a man who loves his job, as Colonel Wigg says, and who puts his heart into every minute.

So Arkle made his first journey to England along with Bray Flame and they stayed very nearly a year till the time came when the Duchess invited Tom Dreaper over to choose which of the two he'd take to train for her.

Both were pulled out: the handsome chestnut and the still lean Arkle. And Tom Dreaper thought about the breeding of the chestnut: the sires were good, all right, but the mares in the pedigree had produced no winners at all. Tom Dreaper said, 'Blood is thicker than water. I'll take Arkle. I've had all his relations.'

So Willie O'Grady took Bray Flame whom the Duchess renamed Brae Flame to give him more a tang of the Highlands than a whiff of the Irish Sea. He didn't run till February 3rd, 1962, when he appeared ridden by 'Tos' Taaffe in a maiden hurdle (by which time Arkle had run three times and won once). He made no show in the race, developed leg trouble and didn't run again. His value? Almost nothing. Tom Dreaper had made another reasonably good choice . . .

Five

AFTER THE summertime young 'chasers, like pink schoolboys, join the training stables which – if they are good – will remain their lodgings for nine to ten months of many years: the other months are their green-grass-summer holidays.

Like the new entry to a boarding school, they are scrutinised by the staff at all levels, and if their build doesn't proclaim athleticism or their eye signal intelligence, these first impressions spark caustic comment in the Common Room atmosphere of leathery tack-rooms. 'Cor! Look what the Guvnor's bought now!' I overheard one of my lads venting his disgust. 'It's a flaming bean pole! Only hope its ruddy owner is quick on the "dropsie".'

It would be cynical to suggest that stable staff measure owners only by the frequency with which the folding stuff glides from clean to grubby palm on stable visits. Friendly owners are always popular. Friendly owners with horses which win and who also frequently 'drop' are eagerly sought after, when the new intake of horses is being allocated to the lads who will 'do' them.

In August, 1961, Arkle and Ben Stack, both belonging to the Duchess, both named by her after two mountains which soar above her Sutherland estate, near Lairg, arrived from England at Tom Dreaper's stables in Co. Dublin. For the rest of their first season they were generally thought of as a pair, being of the same age and in the same ownership. At first sight Ben Stack looked the better proposition, and indeed he turned out to be such a good horse that only something extra special could have exceeded him. He didn't run till December 27th – unplaced in a bumper at Leopardstown – but by June 2nd had won two handicap hurdles and been placed twice from nine starts.

The lad to whom Arkle was alloted had not long been in racing.

Johnny Lumley had joined the stables only a few months earlier in 1961, having started his working life in a jewellers shop in Dublin, after being at 'Swords Tec' – the Technical School at Swords – a largish village seven miles from Kilsallaghan. Neither of his parents rode, but his mother's father had been a stableman – a jockey with, as Betty Dreaper recalls, 'the most superb language!' Johnny worked for a year in the jewellers shop, then packed it in. 'I didn't like the smell of the air there in Dublin!' He came to Mr. Dreaper after a few months on a local farm mainly because he lived with his parents a mile and a half up the road. He did not then, and does not now, amazingly, ride at all. I asked whether he'd never wanted to ride. 'If I had, I suppose I would have started.'

The name Lumley is not a common one in Ireland and young Johnny, twenty-one in June 1966, doesn't look like a typical Irish racing lad. Bigger than most, he is dark-haired with a sallow skin and very quiet.

For the first few months he was learning the rudiments of stablecraft: to muck out, to make a bed, to hay, to water, to do a horse over, to set fair his box, to pick out his feet, to clean every part of him from his nostrils backwards, to put on his rugs firmly and comfortably. Then he was allotted the first three horses he would 'do'.

The labour in Tom Dreaper's stables is about the best in all the Irish jumping establishments and it is very sensibly deployed. Quite a number of his lads do not ride at all; others are novices. These do three horses each. A few are expert horsemen, even jockeys in their own right – like Paddy Woods and Liam McLoughlin, both of whom have ridden a fair parcel of winners, Arkle included.

These do one horse at most, maybe none, but they will do all the riding – if necessary three 'Lots' a day. This method approaches the efficient American system under which race-horses are only cared for by powerful, heavy negroes, who can give them a thorough 'strapping' – the stimulation of muscles in neck, shoulders and quarters so necessary for toning up the system by dispersing stale, waste products. A 4′ 6″ English apprentice trying to 'do' a big colt is often as meaningless as a kitten massaging a bull. But the strong negroes are far too heavy to ride. So this even more important part of a horse's curriculum is in the hands of light, dapper, polished, highly paid expert horsemen. These 'workriders' may ride up to a dozen horses quickly after each other.

But it is very rare in Britain to find staff happy to do the drudging stable work and to miss the sparkling rides, like Johnny Lumley. Few people could actively dislike 'doing' Arkle: almost every time he runs he wins and each time crisp fivers collect in Johnny's pocket. His job is glamorous, exciting, satisfying and excellently rewarded. May he long appreciate it, for he's in a happy, successful and generous stable. For Christmas, 1965, the Duchess quietly distributed £10 to every single person on the place – old and young, whatever their jobs and however slender their connections with their horses.

Arkle Johnny nearly missed. As he was a very junior lad only half a summer in the job he couldn't have first pick of the new arrivals. The more senior Paddy Brown was given the choice of the Duchess's two four-year-olds. He had little hesitation in picking handsome Ben Stack. His leg has been practically pulled off ever since, but everybody has to agree that Arkle looked most unattractive that August of 1961. So Johnny Lumley was left with the first horse he ever had, Don Tarquinio, a horse called Barnaby D., and this other four-year-old over from Chester – Arkle.*

The two most important boxes at Greenogue are boxes No. 7 and No. 8 (see picture opposite page 128). 'We do usually have some good horses in them,' says Paddy Murray the quiet Head Lad from Moate in Co. Westmeath. The new arrivals naturally

* The treble-chance luck to get the best 'chaser in the world would be enough for all stablemen all their lives. Yet, Johny Lumley, two years later was to get another rawboned four year old to do, and this was the marvellous Flyingbolt.

didn't move into the best rooms. They were 'popped away round the back. Arkle was in No. 21.' And he stayed there till victories earned his promotion to one of the best rooms, those with the same room-service, valeting, breakfast-in-bed, and drinks constantly replenished, but slightly larger, higher and lighter, and with a nicer view. Troops have slept far worse and praised their 'bivvy'.

Paddy Murray and the lads are quite frank: 'To begin with Arkle looked the worst of all the four-year-olds who arrived that season. He was unfurnished. And he moved bad.'

Pat Taaffe puts it even more strongly. Twice a week he used to drive over in the autumn to school the horses; and while there, he'd examine the new additions. To the stable jockey the quality of each autumn's recruits is even more important than to the stable staff. The pleasure or pain of the jockey for years ahead depends on the competence and wisdom of these gauche new boys. And their ability can make a difference to the jockey of several thousand pounds a year. So Pat Taaffe looked carefully at the Duchess's pair. Arkle stuck in his mind. 'He moved so terribly behind, you could drive a wheelbarrow right through between his hindlegs!' Take heart then, all owners of hideous young waddlers.

Paddy Murray in 1966 had been at Greenogue for twenty-four years. He came as a young lad in 1942 to 'do his two'. He'd been with horses 'in a place or two before that, but they weren't *great* horses, y'know.' He moved quietly up in seniority, and there is no need to praise him as Head Man. No stable wins races without an excellent Head Lad. Greenogue wins most of the best races . . .

Like most Head Lads, Paddy Murray does all the feeding. 'I'm the first man stirring in the yard about 7.20 or 7.15 – dependin' on the humour I'm in!' And he's round the Yard then with the first feeds – 'about 4 lb. of oats, just a little bruised.' The ordinary Lads don't come on till 8.20, which is when Johnny Lumley first sees Arkle each morning. Paddy Murray is last man round, too, giving all the horses their fourth and last feed of the day at 8.30 in the evening, three and a half hours after the lads have knocked off.

Except where the trainer himself feeds, the Head Lad's value is paramount in a stable. With right feeding anything can be done and only the man in daily touch with his animals knows by feel and experience and intuition how to grade and mix. Many big stables after several years of success, suddenly have two or three poor seasons. Racing men wag their heads puzzling, droop shifty eyes and mutter scandal out of twisted mouths. The loss of form is likely to be ascribed to the trainer drinking, or going broke, or to his wife becoming a nymphomaniac. Something about horses themselves, spurred by the riding of them and eased by the fiery flow of alcohol all day at the races, makes the adultery rate of racing people rather high.

Absence of winners can be blamed on bad gallop conditions, or inferior oats, or the loss of a mysterious magic bottle. But nearly always a sudden prolonged loss of form in a stable is due to the one basic cause, usually overlooked: the good Head Lad has left.

Paddy Murray's programme of feeding in Tom Dreaper's yard is unusual, but most successful. After the 7.20 a.m. first 4 lb. feed of dry oats, the second ('Midday') feed is at 11.40 a.m., very early by normal English schedules. For this all horses get '4 lb. anyway and some'll get more.' After lunch, about 2.30, Arkle is done over and given 'a couple of carrots and a pull of grass.' The day's Main Feed is the third one at 4.30 p.m., also much earlier than usual, but then the idea of 'doing' the horses in the afternoon is unheard of in 90% of English racing stables where all staff are off and the horses are left alone from 1 p.m.– 4 p.m.

The Main Feed is a whopper, a great glutinous bucketful of – in Arkle's case – mash plus six freshly broken eggs plus two bottles of instantly decanted Guinness, plus golden oats to the brim, all stirred together in a squidgy, grey mess. (See picture opposite page 144)

Arkle particularly likes what Paddy Murray calls 'his little bit o' mash. Even if he do be workin' next day I always give him a bit o' mash on top of his dry oats, you see, for flavourin'.

Though mind, he'll take his Guinness straight in his oats!'

At 5 p.m. the lads knock off and the horses are left to munch musically away with only the sharp crackle of bright straw, the click of shoe flung out in greed against wall, the suck of water, and the sighs of repletement to orchestrate the movements of the dusk.

Then at 8.30 p.m. Paddy Murray turns out again and pops into the small, dark feedhouse and off again, clop of feet, clink of bucket, slap of bolt, squeak of hinge, and all round 40 horses for the fourth time in a fourteen hour day. Arkle is great, but forget not his handmaidens.

The hours worked by the ordinary lads, although different from the English fraternity total much the same: the later start and earlier end of each Kilsallaghan day means a shorter span at work, but no time off in the afternoons for a quick kip, a spot of shoppin' or a goggle at the telly.

Arkle must have looked an ugly duckling on arrival. The best thing Paddy Murray could say was that 'his dam Bright Cherry was at the top of the handicap when we trained her here.' Did he resemble his Bright Cherry? 'Ah, he mightn't have looked so much like his dam, but he did look like *some* of her family, I t'aught.'

Thanks to Bill Veal at Eaton Lodge Arkle was 'ridin' and ready to go on with – ready for canterin' an' all, oh, he was well broken, I'd say so' when he came to Box 21 at the back of the Greenogue stables.

Patience still steadied his life: he was to have another four months training before he first ran. During that time, after the preliminary walks on the road, the distance and pace of his work were gradually increasing. And, like all young horses at Dreaper's, he was getting plenty of jumping. 'All the horses do get bits of jumpin' all the way along,' says Murray, 'even if they're only runnin' in a Bumper.'

A 'Bumper' race is the two mile flat race which is the last race on most Irish jumping cards. Most of them are for Maidens at starting (horses which have never won any race). All have to be amateur-ridden, and the weights are likely to be around twelve stone. These conditions ensure that the type of animal running in them is the big 'chaser-type of young horse, up to weight, not too awkward a ride, and capable of staying two miles. A horse which stays two miles on the flat, almost invariably stays three miles over fences; the mid-air pause in rhythm over each jump more than compensates for the extra effort for each launch off. The pause is less in the swift flight over hurdles, so there is less time to catch breath, and a two mile flat winner isn't guaranteed to stay more than two and a half miles over hurdles. A three mile hurdle race requires genuine, tremendous stamina. It does not, alas, afford openings merely for plodders too slow to win over two miles.

The Irish 'Bumpers' – amateurs are thought so incompetent that their backsides bump the saddle when a horse gallops, instead of being cocked up clear – are thus a national shop-window for young potential 'chasers. Trainers from all over Britain carefully watch the results and listen to the whispers of their spies.

It's a poor shop which doesn't indulge in window-dressing, and the Irish are excellent salesmen. A horse having his first run in a Bumper may, if well-bred and well-built, be worth £2,500. Should he win his price will nearly double. There are plenty of Bumpers around, but not all that number of well-bred, well-built Bumper horses. So it *does* happen that the favourite often wins his Bumper, with nothing very much in the field fancied to beat him! Then he has had his turn. He is no longer a maiden. Those who ran prominently behind him will, in their due turn, find their winning opportunities and a place in a smart English stable at the £5,000 price mark.

In Arkle's case, he was not for sale and already in the hands of his trainer. The purpose of a Bumper race for him and others in his position is the excellent one of deriving race-course experience without the added risk of the obstacles.

Tom Dreaper's long range objective is always the winning of *steeplechases*. The flat races in which Arkle was now being entered were simply preparatory stages. His jumping lessons continued. 'From the very start he was always a good jumper,'

Paddy Murray remembers, and Pat Taaffe confirms it. This was a relief to Pat because when he first rode him at work at Kilsallaghan 'his action was so terrible behind that we thought he'd be a slow-coach – a big slob. Mind you, that was on firm ground at home.'

Pat doesn't go round the horses in their boxes, but meets them when they're out in a string waiting to school. 'When he came first he was very awkward. I suppose he hadn't matured at all. He didn't seem to have any speed then! But he always jumped the baby fences really well: always too big over them, rather than too low.'

Arkle learned to jump by being lunged 'on the rope' (as the Irish say) over a few small bush fences which in pristine form had been 3' 6" high (extremely sizeable to start over) but which time, weather, and novices' knees and baby feet had considerably reduced. As soon as a horse jumps well like this at Dreaper's a lad's put up on him, and he'll then get plenty of ridden jumping all his life. Even now the mighty fluent Arkle jumps four fences every time before he runs. Tom Dreaper believes in regular jumping: 'It keeps their jumping muscles in trim.'

He was a reasonable ride at home and didn't start to pull until he'd had his first race. But he did – as he still does to a lesser degree – hold his head very high and throw it about, so much so that Paddy Murray wondered if he was having trouble with his teeth. 'It was more or less habit, I t'ink.'

His teeth did in fact cause him pain in an unusual way as Maxie Cosgrove discovered. When Arkle pulled he opened his mouth and the bit then used to force the inside of his cheeks to rub against the sharp edges of his upper molars. His cheeks were being cut like this and he developed the trick of throwing his head up on a rubbery neck to avoid the pain he expected. Cosgrove had a hard job rounding off the edges of the molars.

At this point there enters reluctantly from the side of the stage the modest young gentleman who declares, 'My only claim to fame is that I'm the only man to have ridden Arkle and failed to win on him!'

The Hon. Mark Hely-Hutchinson, born 1934, an Old Etonian, a Bachelor of Science, Oxford, second son of the Earl of Donoughmore, was twenty-seven when he started riding Arkle several mornings a week before he went off to work at Guinness's renowned brewery by the Liffey's grey waters.

Lord Donoughmore had had horses with Tom Dreaper for some time, including the excellent bay mare Olympia who in the season 60'61 had won four 'chases, all ridden by son Mark: at Limerick, Cheltenham, Navan, and Fairyhouse. Young, tall, Mr. Hely-Hutchinson had ridden his first winner in April, 1959, and was far from the incompetent pilot he believes himself to have been. But amateur jockeys are the only ones the racing press can really criticise. Carp a pro. and a writ will come ding-donging. So Hely-Hutchinson's 'notices' were rather severe before he was first seen in England; and those of us who saw him win on Olympia at Cheltenham were by contrast considerably impressed.

Though he'd be able with hardship to ride at 10 st. 9 lb. in 1960, he was now putting on weight fast, and had to earn his living in an office five days a week. This limited his experience as well as his exercise. But in the autumn of 1961 he was the only amateur rider in regular attendance at Tom Dreaper's stables, for he 'dashed out there two mornings a week for a short go to keep fit. Cantering the fat four-year-olds was the sort of riding I did. I was starving myself then to ride 11 stone.'

Among 'the fat four-year-olds' was Arkle. 'And I can tell you he can't have been a difficult ride otherwise Tom would never have put me up on him. He knew my capabilities.' For some time he didn't notice Arkle particularly. 'In October and November I'd probably ride three or four different horses for a circuit, and if I'd time I'd ask "what's this one called?"'

He, too, thought of Ben Stack and Arkle as a pair so that he finds it hard to separate first impressions. 'The opinions we had then? I remember Tom Dreaper thinking that Ben Stack, much more heavily built, would stay long distances, and that Arkle would be a two to two and a half mile horse. Of course, they turned out the other way round!'

62

In November the ground grew wet for the first time since Arkle had been in training. On it, his action improved and he was working reasonably well, without being in any way exciting. 'Oh, not at all!' says Paddy Murray.

Mark Hely-Hutchinson emphasises that, for this good jumping stable, the young horses' runs in Bumpers weren't considered of great importance. They were not specially wound up for them. As Arkle showed he was now ready for a run, a rough programme could be mapped out selecting those bumper races which fitted in with other stable plans. Some bumpers – those at Leopardstown, Phoenix Park, Naas, and Galway, for example – are a great deal classier than those at the small country meetings and a trainer is guided in his choice by his estimate of how good his horse may be. The race picked by Tom Dreaper for Arkle's first appearance was of very humble class, for it was the Lough Ennel Maiden Plate worth £133 and run on Saturday, December 9th, 1961, in really heavy ground at the little country meeting of Mullingar.

It's much better to aim low. The first race under National Hunt Rules in which I ran 'my' Gold Cup winner Linwell was a novice hurdle at equally humble Hereford. He didn't run very well either!

It was now nearly midwinter. Racing in England that day at Uttoxeter had been frosted off. At Mullingar on the flat damp track skulking on the outskirts of the grim, former garrison town, now dominated by a massive new cathedral, racing began at 1 o'clock. Arkle was led into the paddock at about ten minutes past three for his jaunt over two miles one furlong and 160 yards of Mullingar mud.

Tom Dreaper's instructions to Mark Hely-Hutchinson were usually the same for all Bumper races: 'Lie third or fourth and see what happens.' The stable did not bet. If the horse could win he always was allowed to. But he was never given a punishing race and the whip was wisely forbidden. I suppose at least 100 decent young horses every season never win a race again after getting a hammering from the hands of a butcher to force them to win their first. Horses don't reason very well, but they always associate. When they associate racing with pain from the whip, they no longer enjoy racing and their value collapses as their happiness crumbles.

In Arkle's case, Mark Hely-Hutchinson says, 'Tom Dreaper knew I couldn't give a horse a hard race, even if I wanted to! And I thought I was jolly lucky to be getting the rides at all.'

There were seventeen runners for Arkle's first race: not too much of a crush. He and the other four four-year-olds in the race were set to carry 11 st. 9 lb., but Mark Hely-Hutchinson claimed the 5 lb. riders' allowance. Older horses carried 12 stone.

Joint favourite at 4 to 1 for the bumper was Lady Flame owned, trained and ridden by members of the Ronaldson family who live near by. She had been third in a better class bumper at Naas in November. Co-favourite was Hal's Son, who'd been fourth when she was third at Naas. There was money for Kilspindle from the keen Bryce-Smith set-up. He, like Arkle, was a four-year-old having his first run. Arkle was fourth favourite at 5 to 1, but this was only because he was a horse from one of Ireland's top stables appearing at a very local meeting.

In England an unknown runner from Cazalet's or Price's mighty stables will always attract some support from punters who reason: (a) 'Those good stables don't bother to keep bad horses so this must be good,' or (b) 'If they bother to come *here* with him, he *must* be fancied!'

So it was with the students of Arkle at Mullingar.

Arkle couldn't keep his place early, but made very good progress through the mud from half-way. Up the straight he really began to run on, passing half a dozen of the strung-out, toiling field. In the straight he continued to improve, but he could make no real impression on the leading pair. He finished third, eight lengths behind Kilspindle, who was beaten a length by the winner Lady Flame. The time for the race was very slow: 5 minutes 3 secs. The three-year-old novice hurdle at Birmingham two days later over the same distance was run in 3 minutes 58 secs. Pat Taaffe, who'd ridden a fourth in the handicap hurdle, watched the race: 'It was like a ploughed field. But the horse really got down to it and one thing it did show us: he obviously stayed really well.'

The form wasn't going to mean much, for though Kilspindle won and was placed a few times, Lady Flame was not in the money again in six more starts that season. The race turned out to be as it had looked on paper: *moderate*, with the exception, of course, of the talents hidden in the third horse. But nobody was at all excited about those on that cold wet Saturday evening in December, 1961.

Young Arkle was one of about twenty-five horses at Greenogue at that time, a gawky new boy compared with those seniors whose victories had already put their names above the riff-raff in the thick black headlines of *The Sporting Life*: the great 'chaser Fortria, Olympia, Daily Telegraph, Mountcashel King. Dreaper's yard was well-backed by bankers: Lord Bicester of Morgan, Grenfell, Col. John Thomson of Barclays, George Ansley of Henry Ansbacher, John Glyn of Glyn, Mills all had horses there.

Nothing is more necessary to a trainer than rich owners who can afford the capital for the high-potential youngster and the crushing expenditure to keep them in training. Nothing is better for a trainer than a quinquereme of rich owners – who are also nice. The combination is rarer than you suppose, and most particularly among the cohorts of the Instant Rich. Those who have usually made fortunes out of world wars and others' misfortunes have seldom done so out of *niceness* . . . Tom Dreaper was lucky to have the stout backing of decent people. But then he is a very decent man himself.

Arkle recovered amazingly quickly from his first race through the squelchy ploughed land of Mullingar. This is the test of a sound preparation. Without it, a rigorous first race tears flesh off a horse like a vulture and leaves him a ribby, dry-coated, enfeebled parody.

So only seventeen days after Mullingar Arkle was moved up in class and ran at Leopardstown – the Sandown of Ireland on Dublin's outskirts – in another Bumper race. The date,

December 26th, our 'Boxing Day', is known in Ireland as St. Stephen's Day.

In England seven meetings were cancelled through frost, and though the going at Leopardstown was officially returned as 'good', Pat Taaffe recollects that it was still soft. He walked over for the first race on Fortria. Then that brilliant ex-jockey Aubrey Brabazon, who had just taken over his father's stable, won a hurdle race, and then came a marvellous treble in a row – all trained by old Tom Taaffe, all ridden by Pat's brother 'Tos'. Pat Taaffe rode Olympia and was beaten by his brother, and then it was 3.40 p.m. and the ten runners were off for the two mile Greystones Flat Race (Maidens) worth £202.

Arkle's third at Mullingar didn't suggest to the gorged punters that he was a good thing now. He started only third favourite at 5 to 1, most of the money coming for the unraced Glyndebourne (ridden by the Ronaldson who'd won the Mullingar mud marathon) and for another four-year-old, Artist's Treasure, who'd been second first time out. Kilspindle's second at Mullingar didn't impress either: he started at 7 to 1.

Mark Hely-Hutchinson had the same instructions for Arkle, but this time he found that the young horse had improved so much that he could keep him up with the leaders all the way. He wasn't quite good enough though to get into the money, but finished fourth, beaten a total of $8\frac{1}{2}$ lengths by Artist's Treasure. Glyndebourne was second so the market hadn't been far wrong, but the third horse was an unraced grey mare which paid 36/6d. for 2/6d. on the Tote. Her name was Flying Wild and in the years to come she was going to be one of only four horses to finish in front of Arkle over fences between 1962 and the spring of 1966.

Arkle's supporters were quite satisfied. As Mark Hely-Hutchinson says, 'For a horse destined to be a 'chaser, finishing in the first four in a Bumper is quite O.K. Of course, if he could have coasted up, it would have been nice.'

Arkle had in any case improved – which is what should happen with any youngster. Kilspindle, in front of him at Mullingar, was now behind. He showed again, but nobody particularly noticed, how well he went in soft ground. Had this really registered his next race – his first over hurdles and his first as a five-year-old – wouldn't have proved such a shock.

Now his first year in training was ended. He had six days to his official fifth birthday.

Six

ON THE first of January, 1962, when Arkle, on that universal horse birthday, technically became a five-year-old, he was still a gawky, backward fellow, learning still, but very young for his age. 'Thin', says Pat Taaffe bluntly.

His behaviour at least had been excellent on both his race-course appearances. His lad Johnny Lumley recollects that he was interested and a little excited at Mullingar, more interested but less excited next time out at Leopardstown, which is the way intelligent horses with sensible temperaments *should* go on. The over-excitable animal can never give a 100% performance if he's been devouring nervous-energy and blood-sugar for hours. 'He certainly can't have misbehaved,' says head lad Paddy Murray, 'otherwise I would have heard about it.' The lads in the dark and tackroom shook their heads. 'No, he was grand all right, wasn't he, Johnny?'

It is not part of a Head Lad's life to go on racing. He cannot be missed at home where he is being chef, manager, doctor, schoolmaster, matron, nurse and maintenance man over all the stables' inmates who aren't away at the races. So Paddy Murray and other Head Lads as a rule can never see their charges run, but, having launched them off with their own Lads and the Travelling Head Lad, they must serve at home and wait and hope. If the race is televised they will watch that, and may often be able to tell the trainer things he couldn't spot out there in the country on a pewter day with rain spitting on his race-glasses. If the race is broadcast they'll hear the result quickly, otherwise it's the long wait through the closing afternoon till the results pop out impersonally after the long drone of football at unlikely places.

Till then the Head Man's like the Wing Commander on a wartime bomber station, he has sent his raiders out and waits with the resignation of experience – that old coat against cold doubt – till he hears if they've hit their targets or suffered casualties.

The next race in which Arkle was engaged was on January 20th at Navan, only about twenty miles away in Meath. It was an unusual sort of race in that, though a hurdle race for novices (of which there are hosts) it was three miles long, instead of the customary two miles or two-and-a-bit. Even in England where there is four times as much racing as in Ireland (one day a week on average) three mile novice hurdles are a rarity. If they serve to reveal the future swans hidden in the gawky goose frames of five-year-olds like Arkle, we should try more of them.

In fact most trainers would believe that five-year-olds in January (though technically that age, they're unlikely to be older than four years nine months) are plenty young enough to essay three grinding miles. Though no less than twenty-seven horses turned out for the Bective Hurdle worth £133 at 3.45 at Navan that day, only four others were as young as Arkle.

But Arkle was only running in the race as part of his education. He had had his two shots at Bumpers and failed to win. He had shown that, though he stayed very well in soft ground, he hadn't the speed to win one: and it was the combination of these factors which suggested to Tom Dreaper that Arkle might just as well go and jump hurdles in public. Once a horse is proficient at home, he had best get racing.

The great Dreaper hope in the race, which was so fancied that she started favourite, was that top-class steeplechase mare Kerforo, winner of her last three 'chases in succession. Like a number of really good staying 'chasers the eight-year-old mare had failed to win a two mile novice hurdle before she graduated to steeplechasing. Thus she was eligible for this race, and the conditions let her in on very attractive terms with a mob of novices to which, in a handicap, she would have had to give away stones of weight.

When an unfancied horse from your yard beats your own favourite, two conclusions flash into the trainer's mind: perhaps your unknown goose has turned out useful: but more probably your favourite has seriously deteriorated. But after this race Kerforo was to win another three races that season, including the Irish Grand National in which she beat the subsequent Liverpool Grand National winner Team Spirit giving him 5 lb.! We know now that Kerforo hadn't deteriorated.

Over three miles in January an older horse should give a five-year-old 9 lb. Kerforo in fact gave young Arkle 12 lb. Not that this was of much interest to anybody until at least 6 mins. 40 seconds after the start of the race. For the stable first jockey, Pat Taaffe, was up on Kerforo, the even-money favourite and out among the '20 to 1 others' was Arkle ridden by Liam McLoughlin, father now of three boys. He was then a young man of twenty-six, able to ride at 9 st. 6 lb. and attached to Tom Dreaper's stable where he did one horse and rode all the main work with Paddy Woods. He'd been riding Arkle at home most days of the week recently and had got to know him well.

At this point Mark Hely-Hutchinson passes out of Arkle's story even more quietly than he entered it. He was putting back weight tremendously fast to match his size. He was hard at work in the greatest business in all southern Ireland, the making of marvellous stout. He was about to get married. Quite quickly race-riding became only a closed file in his life. Talking to him four years after he stopped, you get the impression that he is faintly astonished he ever did it all.

Pat Taaffe had not ridden Arkle at home nearly as much as Liam McLoughlin and what he'd seen of the horse by no means impressed him, as he's big and frank enough now to admit. 'He was very thin looking.' He was also, thought Pat, very 'green', and as he was going into Navan races he ran into the Duchess and told her as much.

It would be a fair time yet, he thought, before Arkle would be winning. Of her two youngsters he was sure that Ben Stack was going to collect pretty soon. He was in fact strongly fancied to win the last race that very day at Navan – another two mile Bumper race – in which he was to be ridden by Mr. A. Cameron.

The ground at Navan was desperately heavy and the wind cut across the stands, for the winning post is at the top of the hill. Mrs. Pat Taaffe, formerly Miss Molly Lyons, the daughter of one veterinary surgeon and sister to three more, remembers well how cold it was that January Saturday.

The stable immediately hit form when Last Link ridden by Paddy Woods easily won the three mile chase for Tom Dreaper at odds-on. But Liam McLoughlin was unplaced on The Little Horse. Pat Taaffe rode the great old 'chaser Fortria in the big handicap hurdle, but he wasn't very fancied and faded out four hurdles from home.

When the twenty-seven runners crowded the windy paddock for the Bective Hurdle it seemed Tom Dreaper had a great chance of a double – with Kerforo, of course. The field squelched away at 3.45 on their long plod.

Since there was no doubt about Kerforo's stamina, Pat Taaffe had the mare well up in the leading division all the way. The unfancied Arkle, having his first sight of racecourse hurdles, was being ridden carefully along by Liam McLoughlin towards the back of the main squadron of the field.

A novice jumper first time out requires some restraint plus a clear sight of the obstacles, because the excitement of a race, the distraction of other runners, the clash of hurdles, and the wads of flying mud can upset the beginner's judgement. McLoughlin was giving young Arkle a right good ride: 'the horse's jumping was superb!' he recollects.

Another horse up in the leading division with Pat Taaffe and Kerforo was Lord Fermoy's useful 'chaser Blunt's Cross ridden by Lord Patrick Beresford, a top class polo player who could, had he been as light and small as his brother the Marquis of Waterford, have developed into a first rate amateur rider. Entering the last three-quarter mile Kerforo and Blunt's Cross began to emerge from the leading division, and four flights from home Pat Taaffe pushed his mare's head in front and began to ride hard for home. Lord Patrick on Blunt's Cross kept with him, drew up to him at the second last flight of hurdles, landed in front and began to draw away. To the commentator, the crowd, and Lord Patrick it seemed that Blunt's Cross was about to win the race.

And then Pat Taaffe, still plugging away on Kerforo, saw to his surprise another horse 'absolutely *cruising* past me'. He was utterly astonished to see the mud-splotched yellow of the Duchess's colours and Liam McLoughlin's face, and then Arkle was by and racing after Blunt's Cross.

Now Lord Patrick had the shock. Pushing on towards the gradually approaching winning post – and how far it always is at the end of a race in the mud – Arkle was on and past him and gone, and here was the post and the race was over.

A 20 to 1 winner is never greeted with tumultuous applause. Victory by the unfancied runner of two from the same stable is often unsettling, sometimes disturbing and – in a big betting stable – downright disgusting. I saw a 'hot' trainer in the winners enclosure at Cheltenham once and he seemed to be crying and his jockey was scarlet and his wife looked like Lady Macbeth; their outsider-of-two winner hadn't been 'wanted' that day.

The Dreapers don't bet, so when the first astonishment was over and they'd stopped wondering whether Kerforo was all right and how on earth this gawky novice had ever come to beat her, they were absolutely delighted. And the Duchess, of course, was thrilled.

Liam McLoughlin reported to her in the unsaddling enclosure that when he entered the final straight 'he could feel Arkle travelling terrible well. So I gave him a kick and he just went through them *easy*. Easy – just like that!'

Four years afterwards Pat Taaffe still looks bewildered. 'When he came past me he was flying. *We* were at the end of the race. It was as if *he'd* just started!'

Arkle had opened his winning account. His £133 would pay his training fees for a couple of months and he had certainly proved that over a distance, over obstacles, in soft ground he was worth his purchase price and the cost of his keep. The Tote paid out to the second-sighted handful who'd risked 2/6d. the delightful dividend of £6 4s. 6d. It seems quite ludicrous now. Quite a number of more cautious and perspicacious persons must, however, have reckoned he could run into a place; Tote return for a place was merely 13/- to 2/6d., slightly worse than a quarter of the odds of his 20 to 1 starting price.

Paddy Murray reflects: 'We had a good one in it – Kerforo – and when he beat her I t'aught he was somet'in' out the ordinary, to tell you the truth.' But it wasn't going to be till the very end of the year when Arkle would have his first run over fences and his first run in England, that Paddy Murray thought 'he might win a Gold Cup then'. More of that later. Arkle 20 to 1 anywhere! At Navan!

There was now no time to delay. The Duchess of West-minster's other four-year-old, good-looking Ben Stack was already being made favourite to win the last, the Bumper. Another pat for Arkle then, and he was led out of the winner's enclosure and the Duchess crossed to the paddock to see Ben Stack. Seventeen ran. He started favourite at 7/4 but couldn't finish in the first four. The winner was the second favourite Kilspindle, who had been second when Arkle was third in the horse's first race at Mullingar, and who had then finished behind him at Leopardstown. Kilspindle thus became a yard-stick not only of the rapid swoop of Arkle's improvement, but of his *racecourse* superiority to Ben Stack.

A notion lingers on among Arkle's less informed fans that from this first hurdle race the sailing was not only plain, but unchallenged.

In fact, he was well beaten in two of his three remaining runs that first season.

Before that, however, Pat Taaffe was going to have his first ride on him on Saturday, March 10th, which was the Mullingar meeting transferred, due to the ground, to Naas. Naas itself had had its meeting postponed from March 3rd to 7th and then – most unusual for the clement island – had lost it through frost. The little meeting took place on the eve of Cheltenham's

National Hunt Festival at which, since the days of Vincent O'Brien's almost total dominance of the Gloucester Hurdle, it's been the habit to run, and usually to win with Ireland's best young hurdlers.

Arkle wasn't rated in this category. Not for him the £2,000 crack novice hurdle championships of the season now in full flower, but the two mile Rathconnell Handicap Hurdle worth £202. It was, of course, his first run in any handicap and in a field of ten runners he carried third top weight of 11 st. 2 lb. The ground was still soft, he was ridden for the first time by the stable's first jockey and he started favourite at 2 to 1. The formbook suggests that he was 'waited with'. Pat Taaffe recalls that 'Arkle knew very little about racing and I really had to push him along turning into the straight.' Three hurdles out he was being hard ridden to improve his position. He ran on strongly, took the lead as they rattled over the second last flight and strode on well through the soft ground to the winning post. He won comfortably by four lengths and six lengths from Soltest (9 st. 4 lb.) and Gainstown (10 st. 6 lb.). Pat Taaffe comments, 'He jumped very nicely.' He doesn't say so, but I think he may have expected Arkle to have been rather more impressive because 'After Navan we all thought him a hell of a horse!' But that was a whole mile longer.

Although he was only just five and still running over hurdles, Arkle's schooling over the baby fences now got cracking in earnest. 'This is Mr. Dreaper's big thing,' says Pat Taaffe. 'There are four baby fences about three foot thick and three foot high with furze held in by a tree-trunk either side. The furze is loosely packed and the old horses know they can tip through it!' The fences are very close together inside in a quarter of a mile. 'For the sixteen years I've been there we've been jumping the same fences. So the ground around them is . . . you know, . . . mucky!'

Pat Taaffe had ridden Arkle over these while he was still a four-year-old and before he'd had his first race on the Flat. Pat says 'I agree with Mr. Dreaper. If a horse is to be a steeple-chaser he must know how to jump even before he knows how

74

to gallop. There'd probably be only *one* horse at Greenogue – a two-year-old say, that hasn't jumped! And the lads there, those that ride, they're very good at schooling.'

Five weeks after Naas Arkle was in another two mile handicap hurdle, this time at the mixed Flat and jumping meeting at Baldoyle, a sharp, flat, seaside track on Dublin's north-east outskirts. The Balbriggan Handicap Hurdle was the only jumping race that day. It was a good one, too: worth £387 10s. to the winner.

The weights ran down Irish fashion to 9 st. 7 lb., and Arkle with 10 st. 1 lb. was down at the humble end. The weight was also too light for Pat Taaffe. He rode Dreaper's good ten-year-old 'chaser Fortria, who with top weight of 12 st. 7 lb. started a 100 to 8 chance of 18 runners. Liam McLoughlin again rode Arkle. Arkle (6 to 1) was second favourite to Moonsun (9 to 2), who finished fourth to Storming (10 st. 8 lb.), Snow Trix (10 st. 5 lb.) and Rainlough (11 st. 10 lb.). Arkle was never further forward than the middle division and the pace of these two mile hurdlers on the good ground, round the quick, sharp track, was too much for him. 'Baldoyle's not a course for a young, green horse really,' says Pat Taaffe, who saw the race from on top of Fortria. Liam McLoughlin says: 'Arkle couldn't act round the bends and we got closed in turning into the straight. We got bumped around, too.'

But nobody now admits to the degree of disappointment which must have registered. 'Chasing was going to be his game. We were waiting for that.'

Fairyhouse is Tom Dreaper's local and most favourite meeting, and he likes to run as many horses as he can there. Setting for the Irish Grand National, it's an April meeting with a holiday-take-the-kids-and-dogs air, utterly unlike Liverpool's grey, urban gloom. It has the whiff of point-to-pointing about it – as has Punchestown, Ireland's other unique spring meeting – because the ties with the old days before the omnibus, and with hunting and amateurs and farming chat and the drink flowing on and on in the warm sour-smelling bars, belong to a splendid, vigorous, *local* age.

On the first day Liam McLoughlin did it on his stablemate, Pat Taaffe, again, this time in the 3¼ mile £2,245 Irish Grand National. Pat rode the favourite, topweight Fortria. And Liam McLoughlin rode the mare Kerforo (10 st. 3 lb.) whom he'd beaten with Arkle at Navan. Kerforo gave Team Spirit 5 lb. and beat him 1½ lengths.

The form for Arkle looked even better when Blunt's Cross (whom he'd just beaten in the Navan surprise) squeaked home by a neck under overweight Lord Patrick Beresford for the 2¼ mile handicap chase.

But there were to be no more Dreaper winners at all on the second day, and Arkle started 8 to 1 in a field of nine for the valuable New Handicap Hurdle of £742 and two miles long. Pat Taaffe rode Rainlough 12 st., second favourite at 4 to 1, and Liam McLoughlin again had the ride on Arkle, 10 st. 5 lb. Liam kept him well up as far as he could and he was prominent all the way and going far better at the finish than anywhere else. But he couldn't catch the winner, Anthony (the favourite) who beat Rainlough two lengths. Third was the veteran two mile 'chasing star Quita Que two lengths behind, and only a length behind him came Arkle the youngster.

Lord Fingall's Anthony, a six-year-old, was just a fair young hurdler. It puts Arkle's first season hurdling prospective to note that he comes out 10 lb. inferior to Anthony and nearly two stone behind Rainlough: a far cry from a worldbeater, as they must have said of Churchill at Harrow.

Liam McLoughlin reported that two miles was again too sharp for Arkle. 'But if it had been two-and-a-half miles I think I would easily have won.' Pace and acceleration were still lacking.

Of course, he adores the horse. If you have ridden the champion of all time you are a god among horsemen, and the magic which exists between any horse and man co-operating at speed becomes indescribable. Liam reflects: 'In a race now, you can be lobbin' along on him easy and you change your hands' (moving your grip on the reins) 'and why – he's gone like a deer! Ah, he's a very easy horse. Easy and intelligent. You can travel the world over with him and he's never worryin', never sweatin'.' It's Liam McLoughlin who usually travels him to England to ride him in his exercise in the dawn of his raceday. '*Never* worries. Steps off one plane and on to another and he eats up everything he gets.'

But now his first season was done and it was time for his holiday, turned out in the green fields of the Duchess's farm, Bryanstown, near Maynooth. All her horses go back there for the rest and unwinding which are such sweet settlers to a jumper's spirit, for the fresh grass to summerclean their taut, oat-crammed digestions, for the sun to warm their backs and the slow stroll across the turf to rest those twanging, hammered tendons in a jumper's legs.

Here the horses holiday under the eye of the Duchess's farm manager, Jack Stewart. Arkle adores it. He spends a particularly long time lying down, flat out, ungainly as a dead horse with bloated belly and stiff shanks, just sunbathing and sleeping and dozing and relaxing. Rest, as great men know, is terribly important . . .

Betty Dreaper tells of the Duchess returning from England and bustling out immediately with a box of sugar lumps to see Arkle. He was resting. He didn't, as most horses will, leap to his feet with a snort. He didn't even stir. So the Duchess sat by his head on the sun-warmed bank and shared the sugar lumps with him side by side as he lay there.

Seven

WHILE ARKLE was having his rest, the horse who was to be next year's British champion 'chaser and then Arkle's greatest rival, was changing stables. Mill House was exactly Arkle's age, and like him too, was similarly Irish bred: by a failed flatracer out of an excellent jumping mare. He had done rather more than Arkle in the season just past. He'd been bought for a colossal sum of money in Ireland from his breeders, the charming Lawlor family (who run Ireland's most hospitable hotel, Osberstown House, near Naas). Mill House, from five starts, had won a condition hurdle race worth £170 at Wincanton (this didn't look much at the time, but the horse he beat was Rondetto), and ended up by smoothly winning a three mile handicap steeplechase at Cheltenham's April meeting under 11 stone.

Owned by a rich advertising man, new to racing, Mr. 'Bill' Gollings, Arkle's future rival was then trained at Epsom by the man who bought him – L. S. Dale, formerly Head Lad to Ryan Price for eleven years.

It will be seen that Mill House, although a giant horse and doomed to be dubbed Goliath to Arkle's David, was further advanced publicly towards a 'chasing career than the light hurdler who had lost his last two races.

Mr. Bill Gollings now decided his horse would benefit from being in a larger stable, asked one of Britain's top jumping trainers to take him, and Mill House moved to Fulke Walwyn at Lambourn. He was going to end the ensuing season by winning the Cheltenham Gold Cup as a six-year-old, comfortably beating Fortria and eleven others by twelve lengths. He was going to be hailed as 'the greatest 'chaser since Golden Miller'. His name would be on everybody's lips. His nickname 'The Big Horse' was to twinkle through the headlines. His plans and health would be everyone's concern. His stature would be constantly and reverently measured. Alas, poor Mill House: during his brief reign he was for a spell everything that Arkle was going to be for several years. And there was something about his publicity, too, which rang a little vaingloriously. Poor Mill House; *he* had no wish to ram his name down our throats and make us look for the new champion so soon in the making...

Arkle did well over the summer and came back into training in early August. He was physicked to clear out his inside and wormed and shod all round and generally checked over. Then he started his four weeks conditioning period on the small grey lanes round Kilsallaghan. He came to hand very early, but Tom Dreaper didn't yet aim him at steeplechases. He was entered in another handicap hurdle, this time on October 17th over two miles and one furlong at the sharp Dundalk track. Dundalk, on the sea and between Dublin and Belfast, is handy for Dreaper's horses.

The Wee County handicap hurdle of £163 was so very low class that Arkle, winner of only one novice and one handicap hurdle off a low weight, was made to carry 11 st. 13 lb. and to give weight away to all but one of the other nine runners.

The public weren't keen. First time out with this weight, Arkle started unfancied at 6 to 1. This was the race, though, that first really impressed Pat Taaffe with Arkle's ability. With so much else not in his favour, the ground was on the fast side, too. In spite of all, he produced a fantastic burst of acceleration as soon as Pat urged him and he shot away to win at his ease by six lengths and a length from Killykeen Star (10 st. 8 lb.), second favourite, and the favourite Gosley (9 st. 12 lb.). It was his first win giving weight away on fast ground and a sharp track and really accelerating.

'Yes,' says Pat Taaffe, 'it was that day at Dundalk I first knew something of the speed he had.'

His previous performances had shown simply that he stayed on well in soft ground and that he jumped well. He'd shown conversely that on fast going round the bends he lacked speed. No longer. And this is what excited Pat. The change in Arkle, his development in those six months since he'd last run, was very great indeed. 'Six to 1 he started,' Pat Taaffe laughs now and shakes his head. 'He was never that price again!'

Arkle was racing again next week.

He was not all that short-priced, though favourite, even then, but this was because the company was a great deal smarter. The race on Wednesday, October 25th, 1962 was H.E. The President's Handicap Hurdle worth £432 and run over two miles at Gowran Park, one of Ireland's most attractive and best run country meetings, down in Co. Kilkenny. I love it particularly: I had my only Irish winner there with the only horse of mine ever trained by anyone else – Con Collins, and a good job he did. But that was two years before Arkle came down to run there.

In this company Arkle's weight was originally only 10 stone 1 lb., but the penalty for his Dundalk win only seven days earlier, raised it to 10 st. 5 lb. Even so Pat Taaffe could not do the weight. (It was about his minimum, at a level which needed a couple of days' preparation for final trimming.) Pat asked Tom Dreaper if he couldn't put up a few pounds overweight. Dreaper was adamant. 'If you can't do the weight, you can't ride him!' Pat says 'It was my own fault. I didn't bother . . . I was 10 st. 8 lb. at the time, I remember.' Instead, Dreaper put up another member of the Greenogue staff, little Paddy Woods (see photographs opposite page 97) who now rides Arkle in almost all his homework and who is the organiser of almost every sporting and athletic event in the neighbourhood of Kilsallaghan.

The contest at Gowran Park looked likely to be a hot one. Topweight was Height O' Fashion, a splendid little mare trained on the doorstep, and who four years and four months later was going to come within a neck of defeating Arkle, who would then be giving her three stone. *She* now gave *him* 23 lb. Among other classy horses in the field of twenty-one were Silver Green (11 st. 3 lb.), Ross Sea (11 st. 3 lb.), Rainlough (11 st. 12 lb.), Owens Sedge (11 st. 1 lb.) and Fredith's Son (11 st. 2 lb.).

Arkle won accelerating and coming away by five lengths from Silver Green, with Soltest (9 st. 7 lb.) 1¼ lengths away third. Height O' Fashion was unplaced. Certainly Arkle was still towards the bottom of the handicap, but the absence of weight does not make a slow horse into a quick one. It's the excess of it that slows a fast one. Arkle was again demonstrating that now even over two miles he had speed and class. This may seem laughable now, but part of the fascination of training is trying to estimate not just the character, but the potential, of the horse in your hands. And if they are young and improving each time and more than fulfilling those pipedreams when whisky and a woodfire after evening stables makes life smell sweeter, then the business is thrilling.

There were two very different reactions to this race. The first that Arkle cut himself so badly that blood was squirting out of his near hind hock. The second that this was the first time he became generally known and talked about in the English racing world.

Even as Arkle walked in off the course, through the trees that crowd round the grandstand, blood was running down his leg and as he stood in the winner's enclosure, it came out even more rapidly. He was to have a routine dope test. Tom Dreaper, pointing to the blood, asked the Stewards whether, in these circumstances, the wound could first be dressed. The Stewards withdrew a little, muttering. Heads were being shaken. Blood was being lost. The racecourse manager snatched up the mantle of responsibility and told Tom Dreaper quite firmly that, of course, the wound could, and should be immediately treated.

This was the first time that Arkle had cut himself really badly. But he slightly cuts himself still, every time he runs. This is due to the extraordinary way he jumps: his hindlegs flashing down either side of his forelegs in the manner not of a horse, but of a greyhound. Other horses' hindfeet land just behind the forelegs. Sometimes, in sticky ground, the hind toe may 'over-reach' and touch the back of the foreleg, sometimes scraping the back of the joint or the bulb of the heel. But hindlegs in ordinary horses follow the forelegs like railway wheels. Arkle's hindlegs come smashing down outside, giving him a longer, powerful leap certainly, and impetus more broadly based for the next thrust, but also leaving little clearance as the inside of his hocks flash past the sharp outside edges of his forefeet.

Mrs. Betty Dreaper found out that he brushes only one hock each time he runs: that of the *outside* leg going round the bends. Thus, jumping on a right-handed track, he brushes the left-hand (nearside) leg.

He still does it, and I suppose he always will, and you may see the marks inside his hock quite clearly after every race. It shows how that awkward wide-legged action he showed in his youth, and which made him then so slow, had a hidden, unique intention.

I must make it absolutely clear, of course, that it is not the shoe which cuts his leg, but the hoof itself, and one can't remove a priceless foot or pare it away. James Flanagan is an expert blacksmith, lives in Kilsallaghan, works at Greenogue for Mr. Dreaper, and is married to the sister of Head Lad, Paddy Murray's wife.

I've been all round Arkle's feet with him and looked at Arkle's shoes and he gave me one for my son. Arkle's feet, as Maxie Cosgrove had noted in his youth, are indeed excellent, and perfectly round. 'Big feet for soft ground' is usually so much hoo-ey. It is a horse's action which determines whether it can act in mud. But big round feet which match exactly are a basic requirement for a good, sound horse. I have had one or two with feet like goats which have not gone lame, but they have never been much use, either.

The foot finally supports – on its own at one point of the

gallop – half a ton of horse moving forward over it like a fulcrum. The old toes inside the 'box' of hoof take a severe strain, and damage to the pedal bone and to thin soles is frequent, particularly with 'washy' chestnut horses.

But it wasn't Arkle's hock-cutting habit, which drew English attention to him for the first time. Racehorses are in many ways like actors. They can appear without distinction in the 'local Rep' of small country courses, but till they star in a big production with the critics watching, no one outside the family cocks his ears.

There was a valuable 'chase at Gowran that day (a race which Arkle was going to win another year) and this included a leash of possible Irish stars. With only one English meeting, a dreary day at Worcester, to keep them at home a number of English observers, including some of that cheerful itinerant circus who get paid to watch racing for others, flew over to pretty Gowran Park.

The class of the President's Hurdle was, furthermore, high enough for several of its runners to be already admired in England: particularly Silver Green, Ireland's most dazzling novice hurdler of the previous season, winner of the Martin Mahoney Champion Novice Hurdle at Punchestown. We in England also remembered how only the breaking of a blood vessel going to the second last flight had choked the grey horse off winning Liverpool's Coronation Hurdle on the eve of the 1962 Grand National. Arkle's success suddenly began to register. Literally, his name now found a slot in the range of proved performers. He was moving on out of local Rep.

This was the first moment I took real note myself. Had I been training at that time I would have tried to buy Silver Green from his breeder, Captain John J. Barry, a good friend of ours from Co. Kilkenny, who had sold us several useful animals over the years. As it was, I had recommended Silver Green strongly, but vainly, to two English trainer friends, and was watching his progress with particular interest.

What was this horse Arkle, then, that had managed to beat Silver Green, albeit carrying 12 lb. less? I looked Arkle up and found that he was related to the soft, rather cowardly, horse Greenflax with whom I had won a couple of small races. Foolishly I did not bother to look further. I did not then discover all those marvellous winning relations out of Greenogue Princess. It did not occur to me then that the softness in Greenflax came from his bad sire Fairfax, a horse of Dorothy Paget's.

But I noticed on my trips to Ireland and in letters and telephone calls from there increasing references to 'a nice young horse of Tom Dreaper's, called Arkle – beat Silver Green at Gowran, you know . . .' He was like a young man starting to make a mark in his career. On his level there were 1,000 others. Of these, 75% would never do better, but hang on in little handicaps, decline to 'sellers' and then perhaps get sold for point-to-pointing, 'flapping' in Wales or Kerry, or vanish, nameless, into the scrawny limbo of third-rate riding schools.

20% of youngsters continue to improve for a year or so more, going on winning, climbing the handicaps, winning better races, until their measure, too, is taken, like the man who reaches the level of manager and there sticks, unable to vault into the saddle of the top executive. It was to this 20% that most of us then thought Arkle probably belonged. The remaining 5% is for those rare leaders who go on and on pulling ahead of ordinary able folk. No one thought Arkle was a Top Person after Gowran Park.

He would not be winning the Champion Hurdle anyway. Tom Dreaper now resolved that, provided Arkle jumped fences on the course as well as he was doing at home, he had run in his last hurdle race. It was time to take the next stride forward: steeplechasing from now on.

Dreaper believes not just in a lot of schooling, but in as many different places as possible. Like the good Yorkshire trainer Arthur Stephenson, and a number of practical English colleagues, Dreaper takes his jumpers to racecourses to jump round when racing's over. With this in mind he sent Arkle off on his ill-fated excursion to Fairyhouse to school not on the racecourse itself, but over the fences nearby belonging to the then neigh-bouring trainer Dan Moore.

Arkle had been entered for a £1,000 two-and-a-half mile novices 'chase at Cheltenham on November 17th, the day on which Fortria was engaged in the £5,000 Mackeson Gold Cup. The Cheltenham meeting came only three-and-a-half weeks after Gowran: it was time to press on.

Arkle was heading for his first – and at least till the summer of 1966 – his last fall.

General 'schooling' practice in training stables is to warm up over hurdles before essaying the fences. This loosens the sinews and focuses the eye. If jumped perfectly, as small hurdles should be, confidence blooms in the novice horse and even stirs in the rider: the big animal below and the little one on top get co-ordinated.

But Arkle, ridden by Pat Taaffe that autumn morning of 1962, made the most unholy shambles of the second flight of Dan Moore's hurdles and came down in a really crashing fall. Pat Taaffe was so badly cut over the eye that he couldn't see properly and had to have it stitched up. He wasn't able to continue the schooling session. Liam McLoughlin took over. Arkle luckily wasn't hurt, and really lucky it was, because Pat thinks now he must have stuck his forelegs through the top bars of the hurdle – a blunder which can prove literally fatal. Evidently Arkle entirely misjudged the hurdles and, through over-boldness, tried to take off too far away. Or perhaps, in a brand-new place, he was looking about him, not concentrating. Anyway, it was slapbang on the deck. Taaffe says in 1966: 'I just feel now he can't ever fall, no matter what happens, and I think that one fall at Fairyhouse taught him it all.' As in other parts of his education, there might be first a struggle, but afterwards he knew it . . .

He was of course, carefully reschooled and taken to a race-course and galloped over fences with his companions. On the November 16th he arrived with Fortria in England – not his first visit, but his first raid to race. He was immensely fancied. To the good reports we had had of him from Gowran were now added fabulous accounts of his brilliant performances in race-course 'schools'. I for one did not hear till three years later he had had a crashing fall in the last few weeks! But that is the way of it at Cheltenham. Most Irish horses come down on us in Assyrian cohorts and the English sheep tremble . . .

The ground at Cheltenham was riding good and fast and Arkle's Honeybourne Chase opened the second day of the meeting on Saturday, November 17th. The Irish were really walloping the money on Arkle all around the 6/4 to even money mark. The weight of it, and the English heavy stuff it attracted, pushed the second favourite Jomsviking from 4 to 1 out to 11 to 2. Dargent from Cazalet's stable was pushed out to 8 to 1. Billy Bumps, opening 8 to 1 went out to 100 to 8, and of the field of twelve only the good Irish bumper winner Milo, owned and trained by Herbert Blagrave and ridden by rugger-player and future trainer Ian Balding, was fancied to beat the bright Irish novice. Milo was backed down to third favourite from 10 to 1 to 6 to 1. Four years later, and owned by Ian Balding, he was a reasonable Hunter-'Chaser.

They were off at one minute past one, Arkle crisp favourite at 11 to 8. Tim Frazer, a decent ex-Irish staying hurdler, first time out and a 100 to 6 shot, made the running. At the third fence, an open ditch, Jomsviking fell, and Dargent was well up there till he fell at the sixth, the last fence first time round.

Arkle, Trews, Border Ring and Fair Tan were prominent in a bunch behind Tim Frazer, and at the eighth Billy Bumps, another Irish horse jumping particularly well, began to improve. Tim Frazer weakened at the tenth and Arkle, 'jumping like an old hand' as a correspondent noted, leaped into the lead. Billy Bumps (Bobby Beasley) stayed with him and led from the twelfth up the final hill. But Arkle was only playing. Turning for home down the long hill against the mottled Cotswold backcloth, he showed Britain a foretaste of his magic acceleration at the third last, had drawn clear in a flash and won with graceful ease by twenty lengths from Billy Bumps. Milo, showing signs of staying on, ran through some weaker members of the field to finish third, four lengths further away. Only four others finished. Hop On, like Dargent and Jomsviking, fell; the rest pulled up. Arkle, so brilliant first time out, had cut out the pattern of his future.

'Arkle', commented the *Times* correspondent of that time, (in my opinion one of the two shrewdest men on the job) 'who was ridden quietly and with exquisite care by P. Taaffe, is a promising type. He won more easily than even the verdict of twenty lengths shows.'

The time was good: $4\frac{3}{5}$ seconds under average for an unextended winner. The money won was £680. The horse was really earning his living.

One hour and seventeen minutes later Pat Taaffe was going first past the post again when the ten-year-old Fortria, favourite at 5 to 1, carried top weight home in the 2 mile £4,385 Mackeson Gold Cup.

Arkle's display in the Honeybourne convinced head lad Paddy Murray that here was a potential Gold Cup winner. 'It was his very first time *through* a country, y'see . . .'

Of course, he was right: each horse's performance must be measured not only by what he beats, but how easily, and after what preparation. Here were two-and-a-half miles of Cheltenham, which is a hard track for a novice, because the undulating ground and the position of the fences on the rises and falls make balance difficult. Arkle on his first race over fences had performed brilliantly. Around the stables at Greenogue bloomed that special glow of pleasure created not just by a couple of good winners, but by the marvellous prospect of many more to come. Imagining how good a young horse might possibly be is one of the most titillating joys of racing.

The plan was already formed in the Dreapers' minds that Arkle should go for the three mile novice chase, the Broadway, at Cheltenham's National Hunt Festival Meeting the following March. All the big novice 'chases here are restricted to horses which haven't won a race before the previous autumn. Arkle's victory in November was timed exactly right. Ahead lay the Broadway, a plate of £2,000.

Before that, however, another winning opportunity existed

at the Leopardstown meeting on February 23rd, a condition chase over two miles. But, due to his Cheltenham victory he carried 12 st. 11 lb. – a mighty burden, for the pull of weight increases severely over 12 stone. Of two previous winners, One Seven Seven carried 12 st. 7 lb. and Hyland Patrol 12 st. 2 lb.: the rest of Arkle's thirteen opponents carried 11 st. 11 lb. or less. The distance also seemed a bit short for him: two miles over fences requires, as we have seen, less stamina than two miles over hurdles.

None of these considerations, however, were of any concern to the Irish punters who waded in at the deep end and made him 2 to 1 on. Nothing else was backed at all to beat him.

Tom Jones from Newmarket had sent two horses across to run: Frenchman's Cove in the three mile Leopardstown chase and a smart hurdler Rubor (Derek Weeden) against Arkle. The ground was yielding.

One Seven Seven, now owned by Mr. Michael Sobell, had won his previous race, and now made the running as far as the sixth fence when he was joined by Rubor. Arkle, D'You Mind, Rue de Paris and Moonsun were prominent in a bunch, and Hyland Patrol now started to improve. At the eighth One Seven Seven cracked, and three fences from home Rue de Paris also dropped back. Arkle showed with a slight lead over Rubor. Moonsun was close now and Hyland Patrol was catching Arkle fast. Two fences from home Hyland Patrol was just behind Arkle and going well when he fell, leaving Rubor to go into the last with the favourite. It looked exciting for an instant as the horses landed for Arkle was giving 22 lb. to this good ex-hurdler. Then it was suddenly over. Arkle accelerated away like an E-type from the lights and put eight lengths between his tail and poor little Rubor's extended nose. Pat Taaffe had ridden a really confident race towards a most facile victory.

The timing of the Leopardstown race came just nicely before Cheltenham two-and-a-half weeks later, and all the Irish horses now drew another advantage from their less violent weather. England had been gripped by frost since Boxing Day, and meeting after meeting was lost at a time when Cheltenham entries need a race in public. Kempton, Chepstow, Wetherby lay crisp and even under frosty snow while some decent Irish horses were going in at Leopardstown: Flying Wild, Owens' Sedge, Winning Fair and Ross Sea were other good horses to win that day.

All next week there was still no racing in England while the Irish went galloping on. And there was still no English racing until Newbury, on March 8th, only four days and including a Sunday, before Cheltenham's National Hunt Festival was due to start. The English, ever in awe of the Irish challenge at jumping's heart, now felt themselves singularly unfit to withstand it. There had been almost no racing in England for nearly three months and the thaw now had rendered the ground soft as dough: just the wrong conditions for unfit horses, who can sometimes scrape by on the firm.

The two big novice 'chases at Cheltenham are the Broadway over three miles and the Cotswold over two miles, run in 1963 on the Tuesday and Wednesday respectively. Both were worth the same money: plates of £2,000 returning £1,360 to the winner. Winners generally take 70% of a plate, the second 20% and the third 10%, so that multiplying the gross plate by seven and dropping a 0 gives a rough guide to the winner's 'take': i.e. here £1,400 less full entry fee of £40.

The Broadway is usually easier to win. The class of horse able to stay three miles is usually lower than that of two mile horses, who go a really cracking pace for the two mile Cotswold, in which, as we've seen earlier, the Duchess had already had her Cashel View defeated in 1959. Arkle might now have set a problem of *embarras de richesses*: he had proved he could stay three miles and yet had the speed to win over two. But it was the Duchess and Dreaper who had *les richesses*: Ben Stack, a good winner in his last two races, was ready to win the Cotswold for them.

So many entries had been made for the Gloucester Hurdle run on the first day and there had been so little racing to discard the chaff that it was divided into three. This meant seven races on Cheltenham's opening day of which Arkle's was the sixth at 4.40 p.m.

The English had been dourly beating off the picked squads of Irish raiders in ground which could hardly have been softer and proved raceable. Not far away at Worcester the course was white and elegant with swimming swans.

In the first race, Ireland's best was Bahrain – just beaten by Fred Rimell's Honour Bound. In the next, England's Sandy Abbot contrived by one short head to keep the two mile Champion Chase from odds-on Scottish Memories. In the four mile National Hunt Chase, King Pin, the Irish favourite, could only finish fourth to Time. In the fourth race the Duchess of Westminster's Willow King, trained by Tom Dreaper and ridden by Liam McLoughlin, was an uneasy favourite, could not improve in the last half mile and finished out of the first three, sixth to Team Spirit. And in the second division of the Gloucester Hurdle, Ireland's great hope, Osberstown Squire (bred by the Lawlors, who bred Mill House) was beaten into fifth place by Buona Notte, who was to become another of only four horses to finish in front of Arkle over fences between 1962 and the end of the 1965/66 season.

All these Irish hopes had started favourite for their races, but their consecutive defeats seemed only to spur Arkle's punters to even deeper plunging – like drunkards to the sickening bottle. He was the shout all over Cheltenham that day, as he'd been the talk since Leopardstown and the murmur since Gowran Park. 'Sure, wasn't he the best t'ing from Oireland t'e whole of t'e meetin'?'

In they jumped, English and Irish alike chasing the money gone down on the four favourites before. A few lucky punters obtained some 2 to 1 on before the pouring money made him 9 to 4 on. The fact that he was the only horse carrying 12 st. 4 lb. in almost prohibitive going, was no sort of deterrent. Jomsviking, who had won two hurdle races since falling in Arkle's Honeybourne Chase here in November, started second favourite at 11 to 2. Billy Bumps was 10 to 1 and Border Flight and Brasher (whom Arkle was to meet again) were 100 to 6.

They went off round the New Course at 4.41 p.m. with Boutinskino, then Brasher, making the running, and Arkle pulling like a steam-engine just behind. Jomsviking (11 st. 8 lb.: Jeff King) made a mistake at the fifth fence. At half way Pat Taaffe let out a reef and Arkle darted forward to lie second to Brasher (11 st. 8 lb.: J. Fitzgerald) in which position he was again restrained round the top of the far hill, and leftwards, down towards the dip. At the third last, hurtling down the hill, Arkle took the lead from Brasher. Here Jomsviking made another error as he closed with the favourite which checked his run. But at the second last they landed all four feet in a row. Then a gasp went up: as if Pat Taaffe had only been using three of five gears in a Ferrari, he suddenly shot Arkle forward and the horse came away further and further and over the last and up the hill with mocking ease to win by twenty lengths. It was a fantastic performance. Jomsviking, Brasher four lengths further away, and Border Flight another six lengths, seemed simply to plod on like hunters. Yet with Arkle out of it, it would have been a gripping finish – a reflection which was going to occur more and more often in the ensuing years.

Arkle was now the West End star. His notices glowed. He was sufficiently important for tales of his early years to be hurriedly scrawled on racecards and overheard in bars. Elements of truth filtered through the excitement. Lt. Col. Tom Nickalls of *The Sporting Life*, a man whose judgements, though sometimes necessarily hasty, are usually extremely shrewd put his confidence in the six-year-old slap on the paper! 'As he seems likely to become a Gold Cup winner next year . . .'

Two days later, he could not have been half so confident, for on the Thursday, in the Gold Cup of 1963, Mill House, firm favourite at 7 to 2, gave Tom Dreaper's Fortria and Pat Taaffe a total hiding. Fulke Walwyn's 'Big Horse', jumping superbly, went clear at the second last, and Fortria chased him vainly for the last three-quarters of a mile to finish twelve lengths behind. It wasn't, with hindsight, a marvellous Gold Cup, but it set the critics burbling about this new handsome, brilliant six-year-old star who had developed several stone in the last year. This was not surprising: his size was so enormous that it is rather marvellous that he had run at all as a four-year-old, let alone won. It was this size coupled with speed and balance that set Mill House apart from ordinary horses. Those of us who watched him win the Gold Cup of 1963 could not doubt that we had seen somthing quite outstanding, for Fortria, though getting on, was a solid form horse in the top class, and Mill House had made him look like a pensioner.

'Mill House will outdo even Golden Miller' was heard on every side, and his owner's confidence and predictions knew no limits. Subsequently this fantastic publicity, whooped on by the odd hysterical writer, was going to make Mill House himself seem rather a windy braggart, and, when the time came for the confrontation, a lot of racing people were going to hope Arkle's David would prick Goliath's bubble reputation. Too much fulsome praise curdles like old cream.

At first Mill House's dominating Gold Cup victory overlaid Arkle's image in people's minds. Then, as we returned home we started to relish the prospect of their first encounter. Arkle and Ben Stack (who *had* won the Cotswold all out from Irish Imp and Another Flash) were travelling back to Ireland, and the Duchess and Tom Dreaper were well content with a double worth £2,720 and the effervescent futures of two cracking good young horses.

Ben Stack ran twice more that season, falling at the last flight of hurdles when close up in the Schweppes Gold Trophy – then run at Liverpool – and running second by half a length to Scottish Memories (gave 8 lb.) in a two mile handicap chase at Punchestown.

Arkle also ran twice more, but won both of them. There was a month to Fairyhouse on Easter Monday, and when it came the ground was good and heavy. Tom Dreaper's annual assault on his pet track started with a double-barrel bang: making assurance trebly sure he ran three horses with all his stable jockeys in the Irish National which he loves to win. Fortria (12 st. 0 lb.: Pat Taaffe) fell. Willow King (9 st. 10 lb.: Liam McLoughlin) was second. And six lengths ahead of him was Paddy Woods on Last Link (9 st. 7 lb.).

Pat Taaffe wasn't hurt, and at 4.10 p.m. was off on Arkle

(12 st. 5 lb.) at 7 to 2 on for the 2¼ mile Power Gold Cup – a chase worth £1,137 10s. Only four horses were brash enough to have a crack and none was backed to beat him. Two fell and Arkle won in good time by three lengths, twenty-five lengths from Willie Wagtail III (11 st. 2 lb.) and Chelsea Set (11 st. 7 lb.) – a rather bloodless victory, but beneficial for horse, rider, owner, trainer and the yard. He had now won six steeple-chases in a row over every sort of distance in Ireland and England. His brilliance was established. Nor was he fatigued; nothing so builds a horse's physique and boosts his confidence as a string of easy victories in whatever class. Arkle was on top of the world.

He stayed in training another fortnight to run at Punches-town, that marvellous, slightly mad racecourse enfolded like a 19th century dream in the rolling hills. On the second day of the meeting, Wednesday, May 1st, John Jameson, who make a lovely drop to drink, put up a Gold Cup for a 2½ mile chase worth £852 15s. When Arkle's dreaded name was seen among the entries by other trainers the opposition flew out of the race like pigeons from a gun-filled wood. Only two remained to run against him, but one was the excellent Silver Green, who had won a good novice 'chase at Navan that season and had been about to win the Mildmay Chase at Liverpool until bowled over by a riderless horse. Arkle (12 st. 4 lb.: Pat Taaffe) had to give this former high class hurdler and most promising novice 'chaser 8 lb. And Arkle himself had only won his first 'chase six months ago. Silver Green was ridden as usual by the tall, thin, dashing amateur who used to charm the birds off trees – Mr. Alan Lillingstone. He rode horses very well, too.

Silver Green was backed to 7 to 4 against, and without something of the class and potential of the grey gelding, Arkle must have been 50 to 1 on in his tiny field. As it was he started at the reasonable price of 7 to 4 on and beat Silver Green and Chelsea Set (11 st. 6 lb.) fifteen lengths and a distance. Here was further proof that this was a future champion, whose improvement, so far from slackening, was still accelerating: another good novice receiving weight had been fluently vanquished, and the distance by which he beat Chelsea Set had extended literally immeasurably in the space of a fortnight.

His first steeplechasing season thus ended with seven wins from seven starts on May Day, 1963. Over in England his future rival and Britain's top 'chaser had knocked off ten days earlier, by winning with considerable ease the $3\frac{1}{4}$ mile condition Mandarin 'Chase at Newbury, named after that earlier star from Fulke Walwyn's Lambourn stable which Mill House now seemed rushing to eclipse. But in this race he did not have much to beat for a prize of £2,488 17s. 6d.

The path of a giant is usually smoothed. In fact, a horse in any class who has won his last race with alarming ease will find the opposition scattering from his races before he comes to them. Trainership helps of course; firm declarations of intent to run in the selected race well in advance, coupled with pulsing accounts of your hero's health and prowess at home – 'never been as well in his life . . . etc.' – enables the terrorised opposition to find other humbler races for their small fry. Of five opponents two pulled up: Double Star, the only opponent of real quality, and Ayala the puzzling winner of the Grand National four weeks earlier (£568 10s. from 4/- on the Tote), who now ran as puzzlingly badly.

Mill House had that season established himself as the champion; Arkle as his most dangerous challenger. They were both the same age and Irish bred, and Mill House had it over Arkle on size and looks. In the Walwyn camp at Lambourn, in the Dreaper stronghold at Kilsallaghan, summer swung in through the thick green trees, the boxes emptied as the jumpers took their rest, and most days as each headquarters reflected on their stars, they reflected too on the greatness of the rival across the water. Their meeting was going to be marvellous to see.

Eight

'I THINK I'm getting progressively *lighter* with the horses,' says Tom Dreaper puffing away at his pipe in the sitting room at Greenogue. We are talking about training methods in which – to those of us concerned in racing – lie the secrets of superiority, dreary incompetence or repeated failures. On either side of the middle band of reasonable trainers there are as many nincompoops as clever men.

My experience assures me that, though no trainer outside heaven can convert a donkey into an Arkle, the *best* among mortal trainers can double the efficiency of a horse once trained by the *worst*. And numbers of unintelligent and unimaginative trainers still comfortably abound. Why not? They are pleasant, affable jokey people and many an owner really prefers having a horse in training with an amusing, casual friend to keeping it with an efficient, but unpleasant bastard.

Among their peers the difference good trainers can bring about in a horse may only be a few pounds, but these may regularly increase his position on the run-in by a few lengths, which are often all that's needed to convert a 'bad-luck-fourth' into a 'good winner'.

More important even than day-to-day detail and the tactics of the month is the strategic planning of a horse's career. A lack of vision with a young horse can ruin his entire career. Suppose that the Duchess had been outbid by an ignorant Croesus fresh into racing like a sausage in the pan who sent Arkle to a small clot trainer who'd been buttering Croesus up, standing him drinks, flogging him tips and promising to introduce him to the

Duke of Snoot. Clot would have wanted to win quick with Arkle otherwise Croesus' long nose would have been rooting through the accounts with cries of a goaded pig. Paying training accounts makes many rich men so sick and sour they are beastly to their executives all day. 'Vat I pay all dis money for, huh? Vat do I see for it, for God's sake?' 10 to 1 on then Arkle as a three-year-old would have been bashed along over hurdles by Clot and flogged along over them as a four-year-old, and with his funny waddling action he'd have been nowhere. So it would be: 'Take him down to the West Country in August then, and try and pick up something at the "gaffs".' And on the hard ground round the sharp tracks he would have run even worse, and with his baboon jockey's bat cracking off his puzzled backside, he would very soon have turned it in, and for ever refused to race . . .

The ignorance in racing would not be half so alarming, if every fellow who has once leaned over a paddock rail, was not convinced that he was a racing expert. And this really is remarkable for not many men who have attended a court of law really think they could be a successful barrister tomorrow, and few passengers in a jet aircraft really want to get up front and fly the thing. But some apes who barely recognise which end a horse feeds know the lot about training.

'Steer clear of Blank,' they used to warn, seeing a notorious London bore appear foaming with false knowledge, and with lips turned up in a greasy grin, 'he thinks he invented racing.'

Tom Dreaper is head of a team which holds him in the highest affection. He is elderly and successful and wise: attributes which generally command respect. He is a public figure and yet a private wit. He is droll and likeable and one feels around him the shelter given to an old leader by a long-established staff. It is a particularly happy, even a cosy, atmosphere in which things deserve to go right.

Nearly all the daily administration, the accounts, the reports, dates of races and the contacts with the owners, the movement of horses, the purchases of forage and equipment is handled with a brisk, smiling, confidence by his wife, Betty, many years Tom's junior, and, when Miss Betty Russell, a great girl out hunting in Co. Meath. There is nothing about the stable which Mrs. Dreaper cannot call quickly to mind and her part in the team is much more important than she likes to allow.

I do not recall bachelor jumping trainers who were much good and the help of a keen, knowledgeable friendly wife can convert disorder into happy competence. Most girls actually love it, otherwise they wouldn't marry trainers in the first place. Betty Dreaper says, 'Oh, I'd still be hunting, if I'd married a *flat* trainer!' The jumping world isn't envious of the flat world in any respect, and the disdain which some of the tiny flatsters show for us is happily reciprocated.

There would have been time for hunting if Tom had only been occupied with flat jobs March to October, and probably a great need for it, too, to balance the summer's tedium. As it is, anyone watching Betty Dreaper in action on the steeplechase course can be in no doubt that she's in her total heaven.

It would be very hard to over-praise her contribution. But if she on the administration and Paddy Murray in the Yard hadn't both been at the top of their professions then Greenogue would have stumbled along and blundered badly in the long months when Tom Dreaper was ill in the season 1964–65. In fact, the flag was kept flying for him as high and bright as ever, and the successes brought about in his name must have helped his recovery.

The whole policy of the training stables lies, of course, squarely in Tom's hands. As a convenience for him the horses now don't get out in the mornings until knocking 9.30. 'T'would be earlier in the old days, before the Guv'nor was ill . . . But now we keep the good horses for 'about 9' and get the spares out first – those that do just want a turn up the road and back,' says Paddy Murray.

In contrast to almost every other important stable in Western Europe, Tom Dreaper's horses are hardly ever out of their boxes for more than thirty minutes. Forty-five minutes would be the absolute longest. A ten minutes breather is often the only order of the day.

Elsewhere an hour's exercise is the normal minimum, an hour-and-a-half is considered the optimum, and some trainers complain that shortage of good riding labour prevents them having the horses out even longer – 'like in the old days.' In my own case my horses are usually out for 1¼ hours, except for those who need lightly training or those within two days of running, and my feeling has always been that long hours of confinement make horses at best bored, and at worst sour. The record does not show much sourness in any of the Dreaper team, and if they *are* bored* in their boxes at least they are gentle with it and the energy thus conserved is all the more for release on the racecourse.

Tom Dreaper has evolved his own training methods, having been for thirty years a farmer first and a trainer second. His career is in marked contrast to his predecessor as Ireland's top jumping trainer, Vincent O'Brien who won the Irish Autumn Double at the age of twenty-seven, his first Cheltenham Gold Cup at thirty† and from then on dominated Cheltenham every year until he forswore jumping and started a dollar empire on the flat. O'Brien's career blazed up the training ladder. Dreaper only began to concentrate fully on training quite recently. It was only in 1965 that he sold off 300 acres of his farm at Kilsallaghan for £51,000, keeping only the few fields through which his horses gallop when his sheep are herded off.

At the start of each season, however, he does give his horses six weeks of solid roadwork (for which they are, of course, out much longer than in the subsequent thirty minute flurries). In most cases he finds his horses will need another six weeks training 'before they're runnable. We send the gross horses out again in the afternoons.' Three months from coming up to running is not hurrying and it is probably due to this solid,

* Betty Dreaper comments: 'With traffic passing in front of them, pigeons roosting on their backs, dogs, children and lads playing football in the Yard and handball against the stable walls, they've no opportunity for boredom!'
† Publisher's note: Author omits to mention he himself was only thirty-one when Linwell won his Gold Cup.

slowly laid foundation for fitness at the start that the Dreaper horses seem to go on running so long during the season.

James Flanagan, the blacksmith, also lives in the village two hundred yards from the stables and has never been out of the village all his life. He and Head Lad, Paddy Murray, are brothers-in-law: they married two sisters. He says 'Arkle is always very light on his shoes, even during his weeks on the road at the season's start. In summer his feet may crack a little, but they're grand feet – an absolute pair. Better than his dam's – Bright Cherry's feet were small, but Greenogue Princess – the granddam – now *her* feet were very good.'

It is all a very family concern . . .

'Arkle,' says Flanagan, 'has always had grand manners. He has always been very quiet to shoe.' The world, his wife and child all seek Arkle's plates which Flanagan makes himself from bars of light steel. They are a good deal heavier than the plates English 'chasers race in, and the one I have on my desk (worn by himself in an Irish National) is almost as heavy as our normal work shoes here.

Beware, by the way, spurious imitations. Betty Dreaper reckons 'there are so many 'Arkle plates' around, he ought to be a centipede!'

Tom says, 'I suppose we give 'em half as much work as we used to, but do it a shade oftener.' The horses work round a circuit about a mile long cut through gaps in the fields. Each Lot usually consists of ten horses, because although there are sixteen lads 'all born and bred locally except one from Tipperary', not all of them ride.

The maximum distance over which Arkle is ever worked is one-and-a-half miles, and the Dreaper horses are not galloped or 'tried' flat-out in flat race fashion. They work in two's and three's according to their capabilities and Tom Dreaper merely studies how a promising youngster goes along with proved 'chasers – they are not weighted or ridden out to measured distances.

Maxie Cosgrove says Dreaper occasionally lets fall to him, as veterinary surgeon to the stable, the odd grain of information, such as 'The Airborne horse came through the gap with Fortria and Arkle this morning,' and from these fragments Cosgrove finds it possible to piece together a picture of a horse's promise. 'Oddly enough, though,' he recollects, 'Tom never did say anything about Arkle in his young days.'

A week's programme for Arkle once he is in full training 'might go like this,' Tom Dreaper says: 'Mebbe seven furlongs on the Monday, then a mile-and-a-half the Tuesday, nothing on Wednesday and Thursday and a mile-and-half-again on Friday. And that would be the week.'

Once the horses have completed their six weeks preliminary roadwork they do not go on the roads again unless they are on the easy list, 'or the fields are water-logged.' On the days when they 'do nothing' they simply walk about in the fields.

Arkle gets pretty keen waiting to work and with Paddy Woods on board he's usually dispatched early. 'He's always anxious to get cantering, but once he's worked, he's grand,' says Paddy, 'and then I take him along home on his own in front (see photograph opposite page 112). If he's behind, then he'll jig.'

Paddy Woods has nearly always ridden him since the season 1963/64. He works in an ordinary snaffle with a running martingale on the reins, normally wears a sheet and has a pad of foam rubber under the saddle. 'He's usually very fat,' says Paddy, 'after the summer, and then he's "heavy" and "footy" to start with – very clumsy. But he'd never try to get you off – never.'

Paddy Woods, born in 1930, lives in the village with his wife and four children in a spanking new bungalow he has had built. He is a great organiser locally, and gets all the young into the Athletic Club. Betty Dreaper says 'Paddy is a very great help. All the stables round here play 7-a-side Gaelic football, and Paddy arranges that too. Our stable is a winning team, what's more!'

Paddy says the weather would have to be real bad for Arkle to mind it. He says 'He walks fast, but he's not a real good trotter. And he does pull when he's galloping. Sometimes he grinds his teeth, and towards the finish of the year when he's really well, he squeals and messes around.'

'Very nearly every morning,' says Paddy, 'when I come to put the saddle on, he stretches out his forelegs and grunts a bit, you know. And that's how they got the story at Kempton on Boxing Day, 1965, that he was crouching down to have his saddle put on!'

Every day when Arkle gets back he rolls in the straw, sometimes as often as ten times and then the number becomes a talking point as lads pass in the yard or crowd into the tack-room. '*Ten* times today!' 'Wah?' 'Five times, he rolled!' 'Did he then, 'dad!'

Says Paddy, 'If he's wet, he'll roll till he be dry . . .'

Paddy Woods naturally adores him: 'The feel of him when you're ridin' – Oh, o' course I could tell him blindfold the moment I was up.'

Paddy Murray who has the feeding of him cannot add much more, except to emphasise the remarkable interest the horse shows in people. There's no doubt at all that he does show off when visitors call. 'He gets up on his toes if he's in the yard and holds his head very high and *looks* at them. Especially ladies,' says Paddy Murray. He ponders, then adds, 'I t'ink this starts from his always lookin' for sweets, or chocolate, sugar, anythin' at all from anyone who's callin'.'

This is perfectly true. The first time I interviewed him at home, he took hold of a bar of fruit-and-nut chocolate while it was still wrapped and only peeping from my pocket. He held it very lightly with his lips while I unfolded the paper and then crunched up every bit. He then put his nose entirely into my inside breast pocket and tried to remove my diary. His nose is as flexible as his neck and he has in his manner the gentle firmness you expect from a decent doctor. He never pushes or shoves rudely like a lot of rough horses, nor does he ever hang nervously back like a wary child on speech day.

When I first visited him, I washed my brain as clean of admiration as I do before interviewing people. I convinced myself I was simply having a look at a horse like one of the thousands I have examined and one of the scores I have bought in Ireland. But there was no denying his personality. A very considerable character fills his frame, conducts his deportment and burns through his eyes. He brims over with the confidence just this side of arrogance which used to be found in the best type of English aristocrat when life for a few was stable: he has confidence with courtesy, assurance glossed with charm. His personality is absolutely impossible to avoid, and I found myself after a few moments converted from cynicism to admiration.

He has about him that aura of distinction which lights up an otherwise dreary looking man, because he is a leader, or which illumines a girl without beauty and transforms her with sparkle. I don't pretend these things were always there: success adds a glow to us all, and almost inevitable triumph has a beacon-flash about it. But there was a suggestion there, as we've seen, in his manner at Malahow, and in his demeanour in the sales paddocks which attracted two such good judges as the Duchess and Charles Radclyffe into competition. Victories, which to a horse mean the easy domination of rivals – speed, in the horse's natural state, is his only asset in the rat-race – have built and built upon that early quality.

It's now the autumn of 1963 and Arkle for the first time – and only time at least until the end of the 1965/66 season – is going to run in a regular flat race. (His two 'Bumper' races, as we've seen, are always considered part of the National Hunt programme.)

But it seemed sensible to Tom Dreaper in September, 1963, that, as the horse required at least one decent gallop before he ran at Gowran Park on October 24th, he might as well gallop for money. Just up the road at Navan, where he had won his first race eighteen months ago, there was a flat meeting on October 9th, and in the programme there was an all-aged maiden plate over one mile six furlongs.

Dreaper is not a flat race trainer and like most of the best in his profession has little interest in it. He had no jockey at hand who could ride a flat race weight, so he engaged that excellent Curragh jockey T. P. Burns to ride. 'T.P.', was thirty-nine at the time, a man who had ridden horses like Ballymoss and Gladness, who held retainers from the President of Ireland and five trainers, and who had won English and Irish classics and eight divisions of Cheltenham's Gloucester Hurdle. He knew good horses. He simply raved about Arkle, for it was no race at all.

Arkle was backward. The race was a gallop in his programme already aimed at the Cheltenham Gold Cup five months away beyond the pit of winter. 'T.P.' set off with a tight grip of Arkle's head and held him back. It was immediately apparent to the watchers in the stand that Arkle was, in Betty Dreaper's words, 'galloping all over the opposition!' In the straight 'T.P.' loosed his head and Arkle came away with ears cocked to win by five easy lengths, which was as far as he liked.

Certainly the opposition was moderate. One does not expect a mile-and-three-quarter maiden plate at an Irish country meeting at the end of the flat season to be exactly stuffed with classic talent. But the hands-in-pockets insouciance with which the 'chaser devastated the flat racers was memorable. And so was T. P. Burns's enthusiasm. He who knew the best flat race horses could hardly put Arkle high enough.

News of this victory rang the alarm in Britain: this young Irish 'chaser was something quite extraordinary. It was wondered what flat races he might win.

John Hislop, one of Britain's greatest authorities on breeding, a former leading amateur rider, and an equally dab hand with a pen, had this to say the following summer when considering the possibility of Arkle running at Ascot.

'Arkle's flat race over 1 mile 6 furlongs was a long way below Ascot class, but shows that he can go.

'The record of the Queen Alexandra Stakes shows a number of hurdlers among its winners. Trelawny, winner in 1962 and 1963, Moss Bank, who won the Queen Alexandra Stakes in 1961, finished 2nd to Eborneezer in the Champion Hurdle in the same year, and other hurdlers to win the race were Brown Jack, Epigram, Vulgan and Aldborough . . .

'Horses whose ability over fences or hurdles is due chiefly

to exceptionally accurate, fast and effortless jumping do not do comparably well on the flat.

'Arkle's ability is due as much to his speed and stamina on the flat as to his jumping skill.

'On breeding, there is no reason why Arkle should not be good enough to win the Queen Alexandra Stakes.'

By the summer of 1966 Arkle had not run again on the flat. The obstacle, as Betty Dreaper points out, is time. He has generally been running over fences from October to the end of April. He needs, likes and deserves his summer holidays. If he were kept in training to run at Ascot in June he would get no holiday when the grass is fresh and sweet.

There is no point either in running the world's greatest steeplechaser in some tuppeny-ha'penny little flat race. The alternative – to run him again at the *start* of his jumping season – is no longer so easy. Win or lose at Navan the public would not have minded; before the race he was simply a young 'chaser (albeit a very good one) having an outing. Betty Dreaper points out: 'But if he were to run now in a flat race in the autumn – because he's famous they'd all back him, so he'd have to be really fit, wouldn't he? And if he had to be really wound up before his jumping season began it would probably spoil *that*.'

But in October, 1963, the problems of fame and a world fan club and letters addressed to 'Arkle, Ireland,' hadn't yet come crowding in on Kilsallaghan.

According to plan he travelled down to Gowran Park, Co. Kilkenny on Thursday, October 24th, to run for the 2½ mile Carey's Cottage handicap chase worth £519. There were ten runners and Arkle with 11 st. 13 lb. gave weight away all round: six of the opposition, including his old rival One Seven Seven, carried less than 10 stone; Silver Green with 10 st. 10 lb. was the closest to him in the weights, but the grey horse was fat and backward. With Pat Taaffe up, Arkle started favourite at 7 to 4 on and men who had seen him at Navan admired his swift advance to fitness. He was always boss of the race, and was pulling hard. He screwed over some of the fences and Taaffe had to take a good hold of him to steady him. Greatrakes (9 st. 7 lb.) took the lead four out, but at the next fence Arkle was allowed to accelerate. He bounded away, brushing aside a bit of a blunder at the last, to win ears pricked, unchallenged in yielding ground by ten lengths from Greatrakes. Corrigadillisk (10 st. 2 lb.: 'Tos' Taaffe) was third a further four lengths behind. Limeking and One Seven Seven fell. Cloncahir pulled up. 'Arkle won,' wrote one commentator, 'like a rising champion.'

There were just five weeks to his long awaited first meeting with the reigning champion Mill House. The place was Newbury, quite new to him, and the race the Hennessy Gold Cup over $3\frac{1}{4}$ miles 82 yards, and worth that year £5,020 10s.

There had been Irish speculation about the weight which the English senior handicapper Mr. Dan Sheppard would give Arkle on this his first appearance in an English handicap. Mill House, of course, must be top with 12 stone, but how far behind him would Sheppard put Arkle? 5 lb. was the answer – an inferiority of five lengths over this distance – and Arkle went to the post with 11 st. 9 lb.

The stands and enclosures were absolutely packed, for race-goers had been licking their lips over this clash ever since the previous March. The trumpets had not been silent in the Lambourn valley where Mill House had been made ready to withstand the Irish challenge. It seemed that wherever his owner 'Bill' Gollings went so did a pigeon flock of reporters snatching up the juicy pieces of cake he dropped. Mill House would win four or five or six more Gold Cups, we heard. He was already superior to mighty Golden Miller, we understood. We learned that Fulke Walwyn who had trained such stars as Mont Tremblant and Mandarin considered Mill House to excel even these. The trumpets shrilled and the drums rolled and we were all mightily astonied.

A strong faction stood out for Arkle, joining the clamorous crowds of Irish who saw in him another Parnell or De Valera, a champion to wipe out the crimes of Cromwell. The giant Mill House would not beat their pride, and the English money flowing on him made Arkle an attractive bet: 3's were obtainable, then 11 to 4, then 5 to 2, as the money came in. Simultaneously Mill House, with no public form that season, was solidly backed down from 2 to 1 to 15 to 8. In neither camp, had both been frank, was the possibility of defeat countenanced. Therein lay the elements of a struggle in which millions of people were to be indirectly involved, after which millions would either crow, or find excuses.

The ground is very soft indeed. The time soon after 2 p.m. on Saturday, November 30th, St. Andrews Day, and visibility misty on the far side of the track. There are ten runners being mounted in the encircled paddock and we have a look at the card and at the betting.

As they leave the paddock – Willie Robinson on Mill House, Pat Taaffe on Arkle – the next backed horse is Duke of York (Fred Winter) 10 st. 10 lb., 8 to 1 from 10 to 1; then Springbok (Pat Buckley) 10 st. 1 lb., 9 to 1; Happy Spring (Ron Vibert) 10 st., 100 to 9; Hamanet (Josh Gifford) 10 st., 100 to 7; King's Nephew (Stan Mellor) 10 st. 6 lb., 100 to 7; and Pappageno's Cottage (Tim Brookshaw) 10 st. 8 lb., 100 to 6; 50 to 1 others.

They are lining up now and you are in the hands of BBC TV's ace commentator Peter O'Sullevan, one of the two best journalist judges of racing in my time.

'And they're off. Off and coming into the first with Pappageno's Cottage the immediate leader from John O' Groats, Mill House, Hamanet and Duke of York. Arkle on the far side, Solimyth going up on the stands side. And a *fabulous* jump there by Mill House who jumped himself straight into the lead! But he's now been checked by Willie Robinson and Solimyth goes on. It's Solimyth the leader from Mill House and John O' Groats and Pappageno's Cottage, and Arkle over on the far side. Then comes Happy Spring and Duke of York who jumped it rather stickily. And Pappageno's Cottage has gone there – Pappageno's Cottage is a faller at the second. And now as they come up towards the third, it's Solimyth on the inside, Mill House and Arkle, these three ahead of John O' Groats and Happy Spring, then Springbok and Duke of York and Hamanet and King's Nephew. And it's Arkle on the far side, Mill House in the centre, Solimyth towards the inner. John O' Groats is fourth. Then comes Happy Spring and Duke of York and Springbok and King's Nephew. Mill House with his great jumping, jumping himself right up to the front every time he leaps.

'Coming up to the next now. Mill House in the centre, Arkle on the far side and Solimyth on the inside, right out in the murk now and quite a long left hand bend, a long run to the next now with Mill House the leader, as they make this turn and make towards the next fence. Mill House going very strongly, that long space-devouring stride of his, eating up the ground as he comes to the next fence. Mill House the leader, Arkle is on the far side, and Solimyth on the inside. It's Mill House here, Mill House over from Solimyth and Arkle in third place. John O' Groats is fourth and now the next will be the first in the straight on the first circuit.

'Mill House the leader from Solimyth and Arkle and John O' Groats. The one after this will be an open ditch and as they come up to it you can spot Arkle's pale colours – the dark hoop, Mill House from Arkle. Solimyth over on the far side, then John O' Groats and Duke of York.

'Coming up to the next with Mill House still sailing away in front from Arkle on the stands side, Solimyth on the far side. And a loose horse hampering Mill House there . . . ! But he's all right, – the loose horse has run out. And as they come to the water, it's Mill House from Solimyth and Arkle, then John O' Groats in fourth place. Mill House reaches for that, but jumped it beautifully. John O' Groats makes a mistake there but he's all right. As they go out in the country for the second time it's Mill House the leader from Solimyth and Arkle. And these three opening up a little gap at the moment as they go out in the country for the second time. Happy Spring's beginning to close it now, then John O' Groats is fighting now back into his position. Then on the inside it's Hamanet making ground smoothly, then King's Nephew, and Duke of York and Springbok is last of the nine standing now.

'And as they come to the next fence it's Mill House the leader from Solimyth and Arkle. And a jump there that really drew gasps from the crowd as Mill House cleared it quite spectacularly! They're pretty closely grouped now. And going right out into the fog once again and as they do so it's Mill House from Arkle on the far side, Solimyth on the inside, Springbok right up there with them. So is John O' Groats and Happy Spring and Duke of York and Hamanet.

'And a mistake there by King's Nephew but he's all right although he's last. And on the inside it's Solimyth but still Mill House just leading him. Mill House as they come to the next from Solimyth. Arkle over on the far side: Mill House and Solimyth and now this long run to the fifth from home. Duke of York making progress. Arkle still right there in third. Springbok right with them. Mill House and Solimyth and it's Mill House the leader from Solimyth. Then comes Arkle. Then Springbok making ground.

'Coming up now towards the fourth fence from home and it's Willie Robinson on Mill House the leader from Bill Rees on Solimyth and then comes Pat Taaffe on Arkle as they come to the fourth last fence now. And that was Mill House from Arkle now in second place! And it's Mill House now from Arkle second.

'This is the third last fence: the last open ditch. It's Mill House from Arkle. Mill House and Arkle almost together there! But Arkle a bad mistake! And Arkle's almost blundered his way out of the race there! As Mill House comes to the second last fence the clear leader. Mill House the clear leader now as Arkle's just going to jump it second, Happy Spring jumps it third, then comes John O' Groats, coming to the last fence now. And it's Mill House clear of Happy Spring and Arkle. Then in fourth place is John O' Groats. Mill House has only got to jump this to retain his supremacy. Mill House over clear. Happy Spring is going to jump it second. Arkle jumps it third. And coming up towards the line it's Mill House, the great champion retaining his reputation. Willie Robinson on Mill House with fifty yards to run to the line. And hats off from the crowd as they cheer a great champion as he runs up to the line. Arkle coming to try and get second place off Happy Spring at the line. Mill House is the winner. Happy Spring is second and Arkle is third. Then came John O' Groats fourth. In fifth place King's Nephew, then Springbok, behind Springbok was Hamanet and then Solimyth who put up such a brave show for so long. Pulled up was Duke of York. And so the result of the Hennessy Gold Cup is first Mill House, owned by Mr. Bill Gollings, trained by Fulke Walwyn and ridden by Willie Robinson. Second was Happy Spring, owned by Mrs. Dorothy Wright, trained by her husband, Stan Wright and ridden by Ron Vibert. And third was Arkle, owned by Anne, Duchess of Westminster, trained in Ireland by Tom Dreaper and ridden by Pat Taaffe. Officially placed fourth was number thirteen, John O' Groats.'*

Betty Dreaper remembers the numbness of it: 'We came down off the stands thinking that Mill House must be a wonder horse . . .' Trainers know the feeling: you have a horse you think unbeatable; he receives weight from another – surely no horse exists who can give you weight and beat you. And you are beaten . . . How *could* it happen?

Of course, the incident at the last open ditch could not be properly seen from the stands. Pat Taaffe reports: 'I was going extremely well coming up to the ditch, and I gave him a kick and he stood off a long way to be level with Mill House. He jumped the fence all right, but as he came down his forelegs stretched right out in front of him – slipping away. It really stopped him entirely.'

After the race a friend of Taaffe's standing by the fence said it looked as if one of Arkle's forelegs went into a hole! The ground was very soft anyway, and it is always softer and looser where horses land over the fences – not surprising when half a

* Commentary reproduced by courtesy of BBC.

ton is driving two braced forelegs into the turf at about 50 m.p.h. on landing.

Pat Taaffe is big enough to be self-critical. He feels now that he may have encouraged the slip by asking Arkle to quicken to join Mill House taking off. Anyway, after that one incident he never again, he says, gave Arkle a great kick to take off.

Mill House's fans went wild with delight and Newbury was a tumult. In the bars Arkle's defeat was comfortably sucked down – 'he was a good horse, of course, but nothing like Mill House, a *real* champion, who'd certainly prove the equal of Golden Miller . . .'

The Dreapers went back to Ireland depressed. Betty Dreaper remembers them discussing whether over a shorter distance – two miles, two-and-a-half miles, perhaps – Arkle might be able to beat Mill House.

Of course, Arkle still had his supporters: those whose view down the course through the murk suggested strongly to them that, at the instant both horses rose at the ditch, Arkle was going far the better and was about to snatch the lead. Experienced watchers on TV *felt* that Arkle was gaining rapidly, going the better until he slid off the side of the picture as the camera swung on with Mill House.

Mill House's faction declared with total justice that steeple-chasing meant jumping fences properly which their horse had done magnificently, which Arkle had not . . .

For the racing world, Arkle's slip was a boon: it meant that the duel had not proved conclusive; that a return match – probably at level weights in the Cheltenham Gold Cup – hung out its bright promise ahead. Mill House's supporters, knowing they would be 5 lb. better off at Cheltenham, started to back 'The Big Horse' in earnest and drove him rapidly to odds on in an ante-post list three months before the race date.

His owner, Mr. Bill Gollings, a man who never lacked optimism and boldness before a victory, nor generosity in defeat, had won nearly £20,000 on his last season's Cheltenham Gold Cup wager. It now seemed certain he was going to collect again next spring.

Amid all the thumpings of argument the person who knew most was quietly confident. A week later in Ireland Pat Taaffe was over at Greenogue to do some schooling, and afterwards while he and Tom and Betty Dreaper were looking at *The Racing Calendar* and discussing stable plans, Pat said suddenly, quite firmly: 'Arkle will beat Mill House next time they meet, wherever it is.'

Betty Dreaper comments now: 'That was a bold thing – a very bold thing to say so soon after we'd been beaten.'

Arkle ran again at Leopardstown on St. Stephen's Day, December 26th. His stable companion, Arkloin (Pat Taaffe), was beaten in the first hurdle race, his old rival Silver Green won the next, the novice 'chase, and only five turned out to take him on at 3.10 p.m. in the three mile Christmas Handicap Chase of £846. One of these was his own stable mate Willow King on whom Liam McLoughlin put up 3 lb. overweight at 9 st. 10 lb. With Arkle carrying the maximum 12 stone, all the other runners bar Loving Record (9 st. 13 lb.) were given the minimum weight of 9 st. 7 lb. We forget that even before he had won his first Gold Cup the handicappers were using the full range of weight to try to drag him back into the pack of ordinary horses.

Loving Record was a decent horse and a lively Grand National prospect. With no Arkle around to cast his shadow he was usually high up the handicap himself. Now for once he had only a postage stamp on his back and he revelled in the lightness of it, and ran the best race of his career. He was really bowling along with Arkle over the last mile and going to the last fence some thought, with a catch in their breaths and eyes flicking between the grey and the bay heads as they drove at the black birch together, that he might conceivably win. But Arkle waited till half way up the wet run-in, and then not only lengthened his stride but quickened it's beat too, which is a hard task for a fresh horse at a race's start let alone after three miles of mud and eighteen fences under twelve stone. The crowd could hardly believe what they saw: Arkle, streaking away winning by a two length gap which would have become ten lengths in another 100 yards.

Willow King appeared somewhat later on the scene and took third prize money, fifteen lengths behind Loving Record.

On the second day at Leopardstown Tom Dreaper scored a treble when Smog (Liam McLoughlin), Flyingbolt and Ben Stack (both Pat Taaffe) all won. It was a suitable chord on which to ring down the curtain on a most remarkable year. Even more pleasant for Greenogue though were the prospects glittering like kingfishers among the early mists of the new year.

Nine

A MONTH later it was Gowran Park again and another Dreaper raid on the wilds of Co. Kilkenny: Arkle ran in the 3 mile 170 yards Thyestes handicap chase worth £899 15s., an established pre-Cheltenham, pre-Aintree test. The handicapper had dealt with Arkle and Loving Record to the letter and the ounce. By two lengths had Arkle defeated the ten-year-old grey at Leopardstown: very well, the difference between them would be increased by 2 lb. And, since Arkle's weight could not be raised above 12 stone, Loving Record's was dropped from 9 st. 13 lb. to 9 st. 11 lb.

This was either very innocent or very generous on the Irish handicapper's part. His dozen English colleagues often throw the reins at their imaginations, guess that a two length victory easily gained could have been increased to 5 or 10 or even 20 lengths, and increase their poundage accordingly when your own horse wins. They never seem to reduce it accordingly however when you are repeatedly second . . .

The ground at Gowran was desperately heavy. Of the rest of the nine-strong field only Arkle's old stable girlfriend, the mare Kerforo, whom he had beaten in that first hurdle race, carried more than the 9 st. 7 lb. minimum. She had lost her form and, with 10 st. 3 lb. was only attempting a comeback. What a measure of Arkle's rocketing career: in only two years and the novice at Navan was going to give away nearly 2 stone to the mare here. And he was *still* improving every week because on 2 lb. worse terms, he beat Loving Record by an extra eight lengths – ten lengths instead of two.

Pat Taaffe kept Arkle (6 to 4 on) in the first two all the way. The early pace was so slow that he loosed Arkle's head. Spring-time Lad II joined him at the third and from there to the fourth last these two see-sawed through the mud at a difference of 35 lb. Arkle then went ahead and Pat Taaffe's brother 'Tos' brought the grey Loving Record (4 to 1) up with a rush to challenge him. At the third last Loving Record jumped so marvellously that he grabbed the lead. Arkle got a slap from Pat, shot ahead in a few strides, jumped the last two in front and perfectly, and cruised home to a roar of Irish cheering.

Tom Dreaper twinkled: Arkle was to run at Leopardstown again in a fortnight – 'then we'll confidently send him over for the Cheltenham Gold Cup.'

The public immediately began to back him for the race at 2 to 1 against. But champion Mill House was still 2 to 1 on in a field which the two giants were now whittling down to a match. Even Pas Seul, the 1960 Gold Cup winner and now top weight in the Grand National, was considered a 100 to 8 outsider against the two cracks, and at least 25 to 1 was available about the rest of the normal animals still engaged.

Over in England Mill House's path since the Hennessy had been equally triumphant: he had made all the running to beat two rivals for Kempton's £4,933 King George VI Chase on Boxing Day seventy minutes before Arkle had won at Leopards-town. He then went on to another condition race at Sandown and starting at 7 to 1 on, won very easily, in spite of bursting through the last fence, and squeezing a cold moan from the crowd a-goggle on the hill.

Four days earlier Arkle, looking marvellous, turned out at Leopardstown again for the three mile £1,671 5s. 'chase. The day started well for Dreaper: his new young hurdler, the English-bred Flyingbolt, two years Arkle's junior (and in 1966 the only 'chaser in the world within two stone of him) won the Scalp Hurdle in a canter. What made this astonishing was that the five-year-old was beating old experienced high-class hurdlers on worse terms than in a handicap. It was suddenly evident that Dreaper had not only Ireland's top three mile 'chaser, but, in the two years younger horse, the best novice hurdler either side of the Irish Sea. It was enough to drive ordinary deprived trainers to communism.

The stable and Pat Taaffe then were in excellent form when, thirty-six minutes later, Arkle – with, of course, 12 stone, started at 7 to 4 on to beat five opponents. Loving Record was not having a go again, but two horses with some class were included: the lovely grey mare Flying Wild, 10 st. 2 lb. (Tommy Carberry) and Vulsea, 10 st. ('Tos' Taaffe).

But the real danger came from neither, but from our Gowran Park aquaintance Springtime Lad II, who after falling at the first ditch, went as bonkers as a Hogg, lashing out at his opponents, kicking them (Vulsea received a fearful blow) and lunging at them, neck stretched and twisted, ears back, eyes goggling, to bite them savagely. Pat Taaffe had to snatch Arkle up in a stride and switch him away from Springtime Lad II just past the stands first time round. Arkle wasn't, however, too distracted. Minded probably to escape from the attentions of the equine lunatic, and fearful lest a blunder would let Springtime Lad attack him, he put in his best display of jumping yet as he and the grey mare Flying Wild galloped side by side meeting the fences as a pair. The mare was going extremely well when she hit the second last fence very low and came crashing down so badly gashed that 9 stitches had to be put in her chest.

This left Arkle to hack home unchallenged beating Greatrakes 9 st. 7 lb. (Mr. P. Kiely) and Vulsea by twelve lengths and twenty lengths. Except for the great one, it had been an unhappy race.

The press encircled Pat Taaffe, probing him to comment on Arkle's Gold Cup chances. Said Pat Taaffe, 'We'll worry Mill House a bit at Cheltenham,' and he must have been smiling that slightly sideways, very modest smile of his, as the understatement of that season was noted down for dispatch to Fleet Street.

Half an hour later he wasn't on the stables' Fort Leney when he loped home to give Dreaper a treble. Paddy Woods rode him.

Pat, starting on Daytrip, ended on the deck. There's no time for feeling pleased in the racing world.

Arkle thus completed his racecourse preparation for the Gold Cup less than three weeks before Cheltenham. He had had a particularly testing programme: one flat race and five steeplechases and although all the races, except for his defeat in the Hennessy, had proved comfortable victories, these had all had to be earned in soft and yielding ground. The humping of maximum weight over fences in deep going will strip the condition off a horse quick as melting a candle, unless that horse is either immeasurably superior to his opponents (so that he never has to be 'opened up') or superlatively well-conditioned. Arkle was both.

Mill House's campaign consisted of three runs, three victories. Both camps were confident: Lambourn wildly so, and the enthusiasm, even the arrogance, of Mill House's supporters was infectious. More and more of the pundits came round to absolute trust in the Lambourn giant, and the British public, who had *seen* Mill House winning directly or via TV, and had only *heard* of Arkle's successes were naturally more impressed by observance than report. The contest was a needle one in another way: in both the two previous Gold Cups Walwyn had beaten Dreaper; first Mandarin, then Mill House had each conquered old Fortria. There was more than Arkle's Hennessy slip to be avenged.

The first day of Cheltenham did, however, start a swing away from the odds on Mill House. It showed the Irish raiders were not only fancied but good and fit, for they won three races on the Tuesday, including Flyingbolt in Division I of the Gloucester Hurdle and Ben Stack in the two mile Champion Chase of £2,936 – both, of course, Dreaper-trained, and Taaffe-ridden. The latter race was particularly interesting since it offered a comparison, via the two mile champions, of the general form of the horses in Dreaper's and Walwyn's stables. Walwyn's Irish Imp (Willie Robinson) was 11 to 8 on to dispose of Ben Stack (2 to 1), and set off as if he'd do this easily. But he was overtaken in the air at the sixth fence by Ben Stack who won with a few

No feed, no horse… Paddy Murray, Head Lad, doing the most important job in every stable: feeding. Six eggs have been broken on top of the mash and dry oats, and in go the Guinness's at the double.
(Ivor Herbert)

Arkle and Pat Taaffe neck and neck with Mill House as they jump
the tenth fence in the 1965 Cheltenham Gold Cup.
(Associated Press)

Arkle with Pat Taaffe on board being led in by his owner, Anne,
Duchess of Westminster, after winning the Hennessy Gold Cup at
Newbury in November 1965. (Associated Press)

Arkle and his Head Man, Paddy Murray, in Tom Dreaper's stables, Greenogue, Killsallaghan, Co. Dublin, enjoying his unprecedented press. (Mirrorpix)

The stone above Arkle's grave.
(Ivor Herbert)

Arkle and Meg's grave in the garden at Bryanstown with the
house in the background. (Ivor Herbert)

m.p.h. to spare from Blue Dolphin and Scottish Memories, Irish Imp falling at the last when lying a hopeless third.

This was a hammer blow to Lambourn's ribs and doubts began to nudge and mutter: perhaps the Walwyn horses weren't in form . . . ? Perhaps his luck was out . . . ? The Irish were singing. They no longer considered defeat a possibility. On the eve of the race *The Sporting Life* was not sure which horse would start favourite. The three-day National Hunt Festival Meeting began this year on the Thursday, instead of the Tuesday, so that the Gold Cup, run over the new course of 3 miles 2 furlongs and 130 yards took place on Saturday, March 7th. It was worth a third as much again as Mill House's race last year: £8,004 was now waiting for the winner. The weights, of course, were all level as befits the Derby of steeplechasing, for this is the race, run over a fair distance and fair track, which decides each season's steeplechasing crown. The Grand National, popular with the public, even more popular with the bookies who live well off it, is only a handicap run over peculiar fences and an absurdly long distance with an unfairly long run-in. Few good horses run in it, let alone win it. It has been a richly endowed lottery, a spectacle and a yapping-point, but it offers no verdict at all on the year's best 'chaser.

Because the power of luck is thus singularly diluted in the Gold Cup, its field is invariably select and small. In an equal-terms contest over a fair course what chance has the second rate? This year only two horses ran against Mill House and Arkle, but one Pas Seul (Dave Dick), now eleven years old, had won the 1960 Gold Cup from Lochroe, would have won the 1959 Gold Cup without falling at the last (and blocking Linwell from winning *his* second Cup . . . I must say it!) and had been second to Saffron Tartan in the Gold Cup of 1961. Although he had had leg-trouble, he was a winner already that season, and was the top horse in the coming Grand National.

The fourth horse was King's Nephew (Stan Mellor) a top-class three mile handicap 'chaser who had just won the £2,870 Great Yorkshire handicap chase in brilliant style, and who by Mellor's dash and pounce, had snatched a famous victory over

Mill House at Kempton Park the season before.

The supporting cast of those behind the two star protagonists was therefore of the highest possible class. And yet, in the presence of the great, their chances of winning, even in this pocket field, were totally discounted: King's Nephew started at 20 to 1; the former Gold Cup winner Pas Seul at 50's.

The weather was bitterly cold, and Icy Wonder, a topical bet for the County Hurdle which preceded the Gold Cup, duly won. But already huddled hordes of racegoers had their backs to the track and were pressing against the rails of the preliminary parade ring to enjoy a close look at Goliath and David before they were saddled. Ten minutes before the Gold Cup the snow came whirling over the Cotswolds and the air spun sparkling white. Then the wind whipped the snow aside like tissue paper off a present, and the sun suddenly, madly, blazed down through the fresh-frozen, azure sky and the race was run in visibility so brilliant that the course seemed lit. A great crowd, including vociferous bands of bubbling, babbling Irishmen jigged in the stands and craned their necks and talked in the quick impatient jerks which pass for conversation in the seconds which stretch out, like a nervous yawn, before the start of an epic steeplechase.

Peter O'Sullevan again takes over by permission of BBC TV.

'They're under orders and they're off. And Mill House jumps straight into the lead from Pas Seul, Arkle and King's Nephew, and as they come up to the first of the twenty-one fences it's Mill House the leader from Pas Seul, Arkle and King's Nephew. Now this is the first open ditch: Mill House setting a steady pace from Pas Seul and Arkle and King's Nephew. All immaculate there! A downhill run to the next with King's Nephew the back marker and Mill House making it by a good four lengths from Arkle who's taking a fairly strong hold. Then Pas Seul and King's Nephew.

'This is the water, number 4: Mill House from Arkle.

'Coming up towards the fifth. Mill House from Arkle towards the outside.

'This is an open ditch now, number 7: Mill House by two

lengths from Arkle, Pas Seul and King's Nephew.

'Now the fence at the top of the hill. And a long run down to the next fence.

'Arkle still taking a *very* strong hold. Pat Taaffe trying to restrain him on the outside, not having a very happy ride on him at the moment. Mill House bowling along in front, from Pas Seul now second, and King's Nephew.

'Coming up to number 11 now of the twenty-one fences. Mill House, the big horse, ears pricked, the leader – measures it *beautifully*! This is number 12 another open ditch. Mill House a good two lengths from Arkle – Oh! he just had to put in a little short one there, Mill House, but he did it so cleverly that he didn't lose any ground, just patted the ground with that spring-like stride of his, hopped over it.

'And a *beautiful* jump there by Mill House! Arkle goes into second place, Pas Seul third, King's Nephew fourth, coming down to the water.

'The fifteenth now. Mill House – a beautiful one there! Arkle second, Pas Seul third, King's Nephew fourth.

'Mill House by four lengths now. Mill House from Arkle – lovely jump by Arkle as well there! This is number 17 and it's the last open ditch, twenty-one fences in all, and Arkle is beginning to close now on Mill House.

'Mill House and Arkle – *both* beautiful jumps! Mill House just slightly the better of the two. And now there's a long gap between Pas Seul and King's Nephew. And it's the big two now as they run down the hill to the third last fence. The big horse, Mill House, with Arkle closing on him. And it's Mill House and Willie Robinson, Arkle and Pat Taaffe and Pat being shouted for from the stands now. Irish voices *really* beginning to call for him now as he starts to make up ground on Arkle. It's Mill House, the leader, from Arkle. Arkle making ground on the far side at the third last fence. Mill House is over, the leader from Arkle second. They've got two fences left to jump now in the Gold Cup, with Mill House the leader from Arkle and a long way back is Pas Seul then King's Nephew. This is the second last fence and they're still both full of running, still going great guns – both of them! It's Mill House on the inside, jumps it only *just* ahead of Arkle.

'Now they're rounding the home turn and this is *it*! And Willie Robinson's got his whip out and Pat Taaffe is shaking up Arkle and this is the race now to the last fence! It's Arkle on the stands side for Ireland and Mill House for England on the far side. And this is it with Arkle just taking the lead as they come to the last fence. It's gonna be Arkle if he jumps it! Arkle coming to the last *now* and Arkle a length over Mill House. *He's* over. Mill House is trying to challenge him again but it's Arkle on the stands side. Mill House over on the far side coming up towards the line and Arkle is holding him. Arkle going *away* now from Mill House. This is the champion!

'Mill House is second . . . And then a *long* gap before the 1960 winner Pas Seul comes up into third place and finally King's Nephew.

'I've *never* heard such cheers from the stands at Cheltenham as Arkle proves himself the Champion Chaser in the British Isles.

'So the result of the Thirty-Ninth Cheltenham Gold Cup: First Arkle, owned by the Duchess of Westminster, trained in Ireland by Tom Dreaper and ridden by Pat Taaffe. Second was Mill House owned by Mr. Bill Gollings, trained by Fulke Walwyn and ridden by Willie Robinson, and third was Pas Seul owned by Mr. John Rogerson, trained by Bob Turnell and ridden by Dave Dick. The distances: five lengths and twenty-five lengths.

'Well, there's no doubt about it now. There was no conceivable excuse. It was a fine, clean, perfectly run race, a clear-cut victory with Arkle producing a fine burst of speed. Well, I'll let the crowd take over as you'll hear the reception this great horse is receiving here at Cheltenham from the crowd, English joining Irish in giving him an immensely well deserved ovation.' (*Sustained deafening cheering*).

'Pat Taaffe's first Gold Cup triumph.

'Bill Gollings in the bowler hat, just going over to shake hands with Tom Dreaper, the trainer of the winner: there goes the owner of Mill House just being dismounted by Willie Robinson. Surely undisgraced in defeat, the English champion just beaten by an even greater horse.

'The two riders agreed last night that whoever won, as a consolation to the loser, he would pay for an airline ticket for a holiday for him, so Pat's got to foot the bill for a holiday ticket for Willie Robinson. As he so firmly predicted he would have to do.

And so the result of probably the greatest Gold Cup run at Cheltenham: first Arkle, second Mill House, and third Pas Seul.'

Little needs adding. The Duchess led Arkle into the un-saddling enclosure. The time broke the new course record by four seconds. Tom Nickalls, in *The Sporting Life*, wrote on Monday 'The ease with which Arkle beat Mill House – who, in defeat, was not disgraced – showed that Arkle is entitled to rank as high in the annals of steeplechasing as do Flying Fox and unbeaten Ormonde (another Westminster triple crown winner) in flat racing history.'

Nickalls used, too, one memorable phrase to illustrate the instant when Arkle pounced: '. . . but Arkle went up to him before the next without having to be shaken up. At once the writing was on the wall and the Irish opened their throats. The pair took off and landed together at this second last fence and we knew our fate when, in two strides, Robinson went for his whip.'

Willie Robinson said: 'They're two great horses, and clearly Arkle was the better today.' Then he added, 'I'd like to take him on again all the same . . . 'specially if I don't have to make all my own running.'

Pat Taaffe said: 'Arkle's the best horse I've ever ridden. I knew we had it won three fences out, when I was still behind.' And *he* added, 'We'll win it next year, too.'

Fulke Walwyn was 'shattered' in the words of one pressman

who'd been backing Arkle since Christmas. Tom Dreaper could only be prevailed upon to say dryly that he'd always thought Arkle would win by five lengths. . .

Both these great horses ran once again that season but not against each other. Tom Dreaper, as all expected, had his eyes set on the Irish Grand National at Fairyhouse three weeks later.

He already had seven Irish Nationals in his score-book: Prince Regent 1942; Shagreen 1949; Royal Approach 1954; the mare Olympia 1960; Fortria 1961; Kerforo 1962; and Last Link the previous year. Dreaper, even after Cheltenham, didn't rush in to rate Arkle as his greatest horse ever. He kept him conservatively in a cluster of three: Prince Regent, Royal Approach and himself. Time had not yet finished the telling.

With the threat of Arkle poised over the whole race, the Irish National Hunt Committee, acting with a speed, foresight, and flexibility occasionally lacking in the stirrings of the English Jockey Club, devised a new plan. The handicapper was instructed to draw up two different handicaps: 'A' with Arkle; 'B' without him. There was one forfeit for both races and the choice depended solely on whether or not a certain distinguished gentleman in Box No. 7 at Greenogue was left in the race at the time for overnight declaration.

So one horse changed Ireland's racing laws to allow for his uncontainable superiority.

He stayed in the race with his 12 stone and six more stayed on with him to run for the place money in the £2,630 3¼ mile Irish National. All but Flying Wild, 10 st. and Height O' Fashion, 9 st. 12 lb., carried the minimum of 9 st. 7 lb. Loving Record and Ferry Boat tussled for the lead for the first two miles, tracked by Arkle. Turning into the straight he galloped to the front and in the end at 3.27 on March 30th over Fairyhouse's soft ground it was that the little mare Height O' Fashion who chased the master home only 1¼ lengths behind. Ferry Boat was third another three lengths back, and, 2½ lengths further in the rear came Loving Record ('Tos' Taaffe) fourth.

Arkle retired for his customary summer holidays to Bryanstown, the Duchess's place near Maynooth. After he had relished a few weeks relaxation the Duchess, towards the end of May, gave a special party for him to which she invited two hundred guests, including – of course – Tom Dreaper and Pat Taaffe. Arkle was in his field and the guests were in the Duchess's garden, but there was a constant paying of homage and passing of sugar, sandwiches, and cakes of all kinds from the invited humans to the equine host. Affection and confections were swiftly and politely received.

Said the Duchess: 'Arkle is a very sociable horse and so, of course, he came over to meet his guests.' As the party progressed, Pat Taaffe was persuaded to spring up on Arkle's bare bay back – just as he stood in his smart, dark, party suit – and to the accompaniment of those happy shrieks which are a feature of any Irish racing gathering, the distinguished partnership progressed royally around the party. The fabulous amount of money then at risk – £100,000? who knows? even more? – was not, fortunately for that mellow evening, the prime consideration. It doesn't always have to be.

Their six wins had, however, won the Duchess nearly £15,000 in prize money. She remarked that she never backed him. She felt it might be unlucky and 'Besides', she wisely concluded, 'Betting is a mug's game.'

Mill House ran once more before he too took his equally deserved, more needed summer's rest. Carrying the excessive burden of 12 st. 7 lb. (Arkle's maximum has often been half a stone less) he put up a tremendous performance in the £8,235 Whitbread Gold Cup run over 3 miles 5 furlongs at Sandown on Saturday, April 25th – the only jump race on the card, and certainly the one which sucked the crowds in. The going was very holding and, after a superb display of jumping, Mill House was caught on the tough run-in by Dormant to whom he was trying to give three stone.

A few wise men who had seen the vain courage of Mill House in his last two struggles wondered what lasting mark they might have burned into the physique (which can usually be mended) and into the mind (which often can't).

Ten

HOPE, WHATEVER its real eternal buoyancy, does make a pleasant habit of bobbing up again soon after the steam of a lost battle blows away. New companies of little daring hopes fall in to fill the gaps left by the old ones savagely extinguished and now forgotten on the far side of the hill. In any racing stable there has to be a regular recruitment, and so, for each sad and expensive flop there's always – nearly always – a bit of bright news at breakfast: a young novice who's just worked remarkably well under the rising sun.

The summer was hardly advanced into its normal grey and damp disappointment before Mill House's army corps of supporters had convinced themselves that the Gold Cup had not been a fair test, had not proved Arkle superior and would be corrected at the very next meeting of the two. The reasons? First, firm fast ground which Mill House did not like. Secondly, the penal disadvantage of having to make every yard of the running. There was much to be said for these lines of defence, and those of us who like a struggle rather fanned these embers and the battle fires of the Lambourn lot were soon crackling quite fiercely once again.

As the new season opened it became plain that the rivals would meet again in the Hennessy Gold Cup at Newbury on December 5th. Each pursued his separate programme to that end. Mill House was given no race at all. Arkle ambled off to Gowran Park and ran in the Carey's Cottage handicap 'chase again, and as usual had 12 stone to carry, and his opponents – two only – had the now normal 9 st. 7 lb. And, of course, he again won and the Duchess collected £741 for a spot of paid exercise lasting five mins. sixteen seconds. Tom Dreaper and Pat Taaffe added about £80 each to their bank balances and the racecourse was delighted by the extra crowds paying to see himself. The day could modestly be regarded as satisfactory. Arkle's runner-up was again Greatrakes to whom Pat Taaffe paid a compliment: 'It was a gallant effort, but we were never at full stretch!' And even Greatrakes had paid his own training bills for a month or two out of second money.

When the weights for the Hennessy were produced (this year by Mr. Meredith) it was seen that the top weight was now the more punitive 12 st. 7 lb. instead of the 12 stone carried by Mill House the previous year. He now assessed Arkle (12 st. 7 lb.) 3 lb. superior to Mill House (12 st. 4 lb.). This was thought by some to be light treatment for Arkle's five length victory in the Cheltenham Gold Cup and suggested that Arkle had improved only 8 lb. in the last year, when Mill House gave him 5 lb. and beat him.

Shortly before the race rumours scuffled along racing's corridors that Arkle wasn't going to run. These were hotly denied from Ireland and it then appeared that it was the trainer not the horse who wasn't travelling. Poor Tom Dreaper had been struck down with a virus infection and was in hospital.

The ground was good at Newbury, Mill House's preparation had pleased Fulke Walwyn, he was 8 lb. better off with Arkle, and nine runners should ensure a decent gallop and remove any chance of his having to do his own pace making. This reasoning attracted heavy financial support, Mill House, opening at 7 to 4, shortened to 13 to 8, while Arkle 'opening at evens' went out to 5 to 4. Only the Queen Mother's The Rip 10 st. 2 lb. (Bill Rees) at 10 to 1 was shorter than '20 to 1 the field'.

For most of the English this was our first sight of Arkle for eight months which included a summer of relaxation. We were considerably surprised by his physical development. He no longer seemed small, light and lean compared with Mill House. He had furnished in every way and we noticed how deep his girth now looked, how wide his chest and quarters. We com-

mented round the paddock: 'He's really very good looking!'
For it had been one of his unlikely aspects that, except in action,
he had never looked half the horse he was.

He had been in tremendous form that early morning on the
course. He had had a lighter preparation than last year,
because Tom Dreaper had a problem: the intention was to run
him again only seven days later at Cheltenham in the Massey-
Ferguson 'chase. Two races so close together in a foreign land
meant that he could hardly be 100% fit for the first *and* the
second. A horse 90% fit will gain the extra 10% as a result of
the first race. But a horse fully wound up, 'goes back' after his
race and takes a few days – sometimes weeks – to pick up. He
had to go to Newbury then 'just a shade underdone'.

The crowd was an all-time record for a Newbury November
meeting and 10% up on the previous year, proving again that,
despite the bleats of grotty bookies, people pay to watch *stars*
in action even if they're unbackable, and that they stay away
from mobs of moderate platers.

Probably because he was over-fresh, Arkle was extremely
pleased with himself at Newbury, and those who endow him
with the very doubtful boon of being able to comprehend
English conversations, will assure you that he deliberately took
the mickey out of the Mill House camp: 'So Mill House was
only beat at Cheltenham because he made the running? Very
well. Watch this!'

The gigantic crowd gasped when it saw Arkle under 12 st.
7 lb. suddenly charge to the front, take off, and keep batting on
down the far side at a speed which looked terrifying to sit upon
and was astonishing to watch. This was crazy! we thought.
He's playing right into Mill House's hands . . . And there the
big horse was, sitting on Arkle's quarters, getting the lead he
wanted. Arkle at this clip must cut his own throat.

Over the water by the winning post and round the bend and
away flew the two Gold Cup winners and together – crack,
crack, crack – over the three fences on the far side. For the first
time we heard in England the sound French racegoers know:
bursts of crackling applause at each spectacular leap. And then

we could see that Mill House was stretching and struggling to hang on to Arkle and that at each jump Arkle was smoothly pulling a little away. Between the last two on the far side Arkle was two lengths clear. Then he crashed right through the sixth from home with a bang that shuddered through the crowd. But before we could even let our moans out we saw the blunder hadn't rocked either Pat Taaffe or himself at all.

All it did was to let Mill House close up for a little, but by the next fence he had been mastered again, and at the fourth from home all hope had hissed away. Ferry Boat, also from Ireland, receiving 35 lb., now came at Arkle with a run which, over any other horse at these weights, would have swept him to victory. But he threatened only for a few swinging strides, then Arkle shook him off. He made another mistake at the second last, screwing sharply as he landed which seemed not to perturb him at all, and he came away ridden along by Pat Taaffe to win by ten lengths and twelve lengths from Ferry Boat (T. M. Jones) and The Rip. Mill House, utterly exhausted, toiled in fourth, a further six lengths back: a total of twenty-eight lengths and 3 lb. behind the new champion.

The decider of their first three meetings was over. There was a fantastic reception as the Duchess led Arkle in, attended by Johnny Lumley and Liam McLoughlin. The Queen Mother, owner of The Rip, immediately came across to congratulate the Duchess with one of her wide wonderful smiles and could be heard to say under the clamour, 'That was *some* race, wasn't it! Absolutely *marvellous*!' Three cheers were suddenly called for, and rousingly given, and the Duchess, overcome, was quite breathless. Her first comment to be heard in the bedlam was her loyal, affectionate regret that Tom Dreaper could not be there to have seen the third of the three struggles between Arkle and Mill House.

The poor 'Big Horse' was totally eclipsed, and it seemed all too likely that his last three hard races had had a cruel effect. As with a man whose habit it is to lead and succeed, so a great horse who is finally, then repeatedly crushed by a greater one, suffers the bigger beating, because he puts all in, and is the more disheartened. The moderate handicapper accustomed to regular defeats does not gallop his heart out when he is headed. Mill House did – and several knowledgeable Jeremiahs at Newbury were sure he would never be the same again.

The race was worth £5,516 2s. 6d., bringing Arkle's total earnings to over £23,000 and was run in 17.5 seconds under average time. Arkle's performance, under this weight and doing all the donkey work, overtopped his Gold Cup victory. There seemed to be a magic quality about him now: already soaring over the summit of any first-class horse, his improvement had still not stopped, but seemed to be accelerating faster and faster towards incredibility.

Pat Taaffe, though quiet amidst the tumult after the race, was quite astonished. 'I was a passenger! I just couldn't hold him!' And then in his slow, gentle voice he added, 'It was the best race he's run yet, but I think he needed it! And I think he'll improve.'

After the race there was at first doubt whether Arkle would go on to Cheltenham for the Massey-Ferguson Gold Cup in which his weight with a 3 lb. penalty for winning the Hennessy had now gone up to the almost impossible burden of 12 st. 10 lb. The Massey-Ferguson was worth £3,989 and was due to be run over 2 miles 5 furlongs, a distance rather less than that over which Arkle had beaten top-class company.

One of the most fancied horses in the field was Mr. Jim Joel's crack novice 'chaser of last year, the beautiful high-quality Buona Notte. He was briskly backed in the antepost lists from 10 to 1 to 7 to 1 immediately after Newbury, and his trainer Bob Turnell remarked at Windsor midweek: 'They may find Arkle could have done with a longer rest after Newbury.' He also commented: 'Ferry Boat finished too close to him for my liking.'

Tom Dreaper was still ill. But Betty Dreaper was in charge in Ireland and she told Tim Fitzgeorge-Parker of the *Daily Mail*: 'I'm confident of a second great win. Arkle's in tremendous form.'

But Arkle wasn't in Ireland. A certain mystery about his

whereabouts – some said Lambourn, others reported he had already arrived at Cheltenham – decked glamour round his hero's image. But, in fact, his owner had reasonably suggested that he should spend the six days between the races at her own place, Eaton Lodge, a converted cottage on the great Westminster estates near Chester. Thither Arkle and his attendants repaired.

Now if there is one certainty about the owner of a winning horse it is that he will want to call on him and fuss over him and discover again how really handsome, intelligent and kind he is, particularly now that he has won. If the winning horse in question has earned a tax free figure which would need a gross income exceeding £100,000 to produce, some gratitude is expected to flow out at most hours of the day in the shape of sugar and sweets and general affection. If the owner is a popular woman with lots of friends it would be most surprising if friends didn't call to say hello to Arkle, to touch him for luck, and to pat him for love, or to be able to tell their children they had stood within reach of him.

So it was that Arkle's brief return to Eaton was, to put it mildly, somewhat social, and he may not have had total peace, quiet and relaxation before he arrived at Cheltenham for the Massey-Ferguson Gold Cup.

Bob Turnell was not the only professional racing man to voice the view that the short space between races *plus* his penalty *plus* the shorter distance might well undo the champion. A few writers, ever mindful of their responsibilities as owners' advisers, (the perfect job: to prescribe publicly without any responsibility yourself) now maintained that it was not fair on Arkle to run him at all.

But he ran all right and started 11 to 8 *on*, in spite of his own disadvantages, and in spite of having to give 32 lb. to the grey mare Flying Wild – co-favourite for the last Grand National, and 26 lb. to Buona Notte who had been the top novice 'chaser of the previous season – the 'Arkle' of that vintage.

Buona Notte, 10 st. 12 lb. (Johnny Haine) was well backed from 11 to 2 down to 4 to 1, and the crack two mile 'chaser-hurdler Scottish Memories, 10 st. 5 lb., (Cathal Finnegan) came in to 8 to 1 from 9 to 1. Peter Cazalet's good 2 miler Wilmington II, carrying 10 st. 6 lb. with his 6 lb. penalty (Bill Rees) at 100 to 7, and Dan Moore's Irish-trained Flying Wild, 10 st. 6 lb. (Tommy Carberry) at 100 to 8 from 10 to 1, made up the market.

Drawbacks did not deter Arkle. Remembering Newbury he again took a ferocious hold and pulled Pat Taaffe forward into second place, behind The O'Malley 10 st. (P. Broderick). At the sixth Arkle fought his way just in front of The O'Malley, but the pair were close together pursued by Scottish Memories, Wilmington II and Buona Notte. The O'Malley was a shade in front again as they came up to the thirteenth fence.

Four from home at the top of the hill Arkle swooped ahead again and Pat Taaffe now started to drive him down the long sweeping hill into the dip. As they came to the second last The O'Malley, behind him, suddenly slipped up on the flat – the going was greasy – and a rumble and fluster rushed through the stands: just behind Arkle they could see first Flying Wild (see picture opposite page 33), then Buona Notte, then Scottish Memories closing the gap like wolves and gaining every second. 'Arkle's beaten! He's beaten!' the crowd mourned, and as they came to the last the grey mare and the nearly-black gelding both headed him. It was Buona Notte who edged slightly ahead as the two drew away from Arkle as they went into the last fence but here Buona Notte blundered, hitting the fence and sprawling as he landed. Now the chance flashed to Flying Wild. The mare should win easily. But Buona Notte recovered, rallied, and surged after her, and suddenly here was Arkle, too, under Pat Taaffe's driving boots and flying stick closing the gap again, and humping his monstrous weight up the grinding hill like a hero.

In one of the best finishes of hundreds I have enjoyed at Cheltenham, Flying Wild just beat Buona Notte a short-head, with Arkle third, only a length behind him, and Scottish Memories only a further two lengths back, 4th.

Arkle, as the press announced, was 'magnificent even in defeat', and there was a unanimous hope that the severe race would not have harmed him, and that he would now enjoy a rest.

The combination of three reasons for his defeat – (1) too soon after his previous race; (2) crushing weight; (3) shorter distance – has not so far occurred again. And the one hiccup in the long string of 1111111's may for a month or two have made a few handicappers wonder whether they were not being too harsh on him. Defeats, as is only fair, do give some respite from the stones of lead.

Tom Dreaper knew his business well enough without advice and it was nearly three months before Arkle ran again.

The year 1964 had proved Dreaper's best-ever in thirty-three years of training at Kilsallaghan. During the year he had won stakes in Ireland for his patrons worth £23,323 13s. 6d. – a total which shot him right away from other mainly National Hunt trainers, and had him breathing down the necks of the top four Irish flat trainers with their much larger prize money. Paddy Prendergast himself won only £233 more than the wise old man of Kilsallaghan – and yet there was only ten jumping races all year worth more than £1,000.

And Dreaper earned British sterling, too. Arkle, Ben Stack, Flyingbolt and Crown Prince collected £18,526 of English stakes, making Dreaper's grand total £41,849. Arkle himself won £19,462.

Arkle had earned at least £2,000 extra that year for Tom Dreaper and Pat Taaffe in their 10% commissions. Pat, champion Irish National Hunt jockey with thirty-eight winners – thirteen ahead of Tommy Carberry – received his fifth successive 'Oscar' at the Irish Jockey's Dinner in his honour on January 16th.

The first race selected for Arkle in 1965 was one at home: a repeat of the three mile handicap chase at Leopardstown, which he had won last year despite the savage attentions of the loose horse, Springtime Lad II, now run on Saturday, February 27th, and worth £2,583 15s.

This year Arkle had 7 lb. more to make the maximum 12 st.

7 lb., but the only runner of eight opponents who looked as if he might trouble the champion at these weights was the two mile 'crack' Scottish Memories (10 st., Frankie Carroll) now receiving $2\frac{1}{2}$ stone – 2 lb. more than when he was two lengths behind Arkle in the Massey-Ferguson.

The handicapper's judgement proved correct: Arkle at 11 to 8 on had to battle really hard to beat off the strong challenge of Scottish Memories (5 to 1) and won by only one length. Persian Signal 9 st. 7 lb. (A. Redwood) was third another ten lengths away. In 6 minutes 14 seconds Arkle earned another £2,583 15s., and Mr. Phil Bull's unique publication *Timeform* elevated him to the fantastic rating of 200 (Mill House was 184) and remarked, without really putting its neck out, 'looks a Cheltenham banker'.

Unfortunately for Mill House things had not been going easily for him since his defeat in the Hennessy. What he required were a couple of easy races which he could win unextended and thus enjoy a superiority over lesser quadrupeds. But races like this for a horse who has recently been the king 'chaser of the islands are hard to find. He must necessarily be top of the handicap everywhere in Arkle's absence, and his opponents, like jackals, were no longer going to be scared away. They saw in his exhaustion at the end of the Hennessy signs that the idol was cracking, that the 'Big Horse' had finished his life at the top. They would have a go at him while the handicapper still had him crushed.

So they took him on, seven of them, in the $3\frac{1}{4}$ mile Mandarin Handicap Chase at Newbury again in very soft ground on Saturday, January 16th, 1965. Mill House (12 st. 7 lb.) had to give Buona Notte (11 st. 9 lb.) 12 lb., and, after the Massey-Ferguson it did not seem he could do it. So Buona Notte (Johnny Haine) started just favourite at 5 to 4, Mill House (Willie Robinson) was 6 to 4 and the previous year's Whitbread Gold Cup winner Dormant, 10 st. 13 lb. (Pat Buckley) was next best backed at 9 to 1.

Buona Notte was going fairly easily, but hadn't been jumping too perfectly when he fell at the fourteenth fence with nearly a mile to run. The tearaway Out and About had been either leading or second up till then, and now Dormant went on. Mill House, jumping without his old splendid abandon, was battling on dourly behind and making a few blunders, but he came up to Dormant and caught him at the last fence. Dormant came back at him on the boggy run-in, but Mill House under tremendous hammering hung dourly on and scraped home, absolutely flat out and staggering, by only a head. Coming after the Hennessy, nothing could have been worse for him.

A month later Fulke Walwyn found what seemed an easier test in the Gainsborough 'Chase at Sandown, a three mile condition race, which he had won so easily last year. Under the conditions he could not have more than 12 st. 5 lb. to his three opponents' 10 st. 9 lb. He had Ferry Boat (Mr. Bill McLernon) to beat, and though he jumped rather more in his old extravagant style, he still made three blunders and was caught by Ferry Boat as they came squelching to the last. This meant another struggle up the cruel run-in and once again Mill House was all out to win by 1½ lengths.

There was no flicker of doubt which of the two rivals had had the better preparation for round four of this duel: the 1965 Cheltenham Gold Cup, worth a little less this year (due to an understandable fall-off in entries and acceptors) at £7,986 10s. The distance was less, too: 3 miles 2 furlongs and 76 yards – a reduction of 54 yards.

The day is Thursday, March 11th, 1965 and the time shortly before four o'clock. The weather is sharp and the ground firm, dried out by the keen, frosty winds which have been blowing across Prestbury Park the last two days. For BBC TV Clive Graham, the *Daily Express*' racing writer, is running his eyes over the four runners for the Gold Cup. As we join him, he's telling us:

'. . . And we're looking at Mr. Bill Gollings' Mill House, Irish-bred by King Hal out of Nas na Riogh' (*pronouncing it Naice ne Ree*) 'and the horse whose rivalry with Arkle has been the most exciting feature of the past two seasons' National Hunt racing. So far the advantage lies with Arkle and in this meeting Mill House will be seeking to gain the reputation which Arkle has tarnished more than somewhat. The ground might be, perhaps, a little bit on the firm side for Mill House. He's shown his preference for softer ground, but Fulke Walwyn has him turned out looking a picture and Fulke is by no means without hopes of bringing off the big Cheltenham double – having won the Champion Hurdle here yesterday with the 50 to 1 shot, Kirriemuir, also ridden by Mill House's jockey, Willie Robinson.

'As you see, this horse has ideal temperament for a steeple-chaser, nothing worries him. He's been here before and he looks as if he knew the place well enough. But he hasn't yet had a look across at Arkle who's just come into the paddock.

'And, of course, there's also Stoney Crossing and Caduval to complete the four runners in an unusual running of this famous steeplechase.

'And here comes Arkle, the mount of course of Pat Taaffe, trained by Tom Dreaper for Nancy, Duchess of Westminster – the horse that was just a shade unlucky to be beaten here, giving lumps of weight away, on his last visit to Cheltenham after that brilliant performance in the Hennessy Gold Cup and that fine victory over Mill House in this race last year.

'Not very often do we find two previous winners of the Cheltenham Gold Cup taking each other on. This race of course was made famous by Golden Miller who won it five times. As Arkle is an eight-year-old, probably he'll never be able to equal the Miller's great record, but there's no doubt at all he's a fantastically good steeplechaser . . .

'Arkle last time out showed that he'd retained his form – that that Cheltenham race hadn't daunted him at all – by beating Scottish Memories giving him lumps of weight away. It's an extraordinary horse this, because he's a very hard puller, yet, when he seems to come to the end of his tether – when most other horses *would* have come to the end of their tether – this fellow finds some hidden reserves . . .

'Now we can have a look at their two rivals. This hog-maned horse is the Australian challenger, Stoney Crossing, who's an Olympic performer. He *has* run in steeplechases in Australia, but it's impossible to relate the form there to the form here. He's being ridden by Mr. Bill Roycroft who rode his horse Avatar in the Champion Hurdle yesterday, finishing last, but didn't run at all badly. The jockeys had no complaints about Mr. Roycroft's riding! He's a veteran, he's past fifty. He'll probably have an enjoyable experience here anyway, hacking round. There's no reason why he should get in the way of his more illustrious rivals.

'Now the fourth runner – here he is – Caduval, a course winner. He's in the Grand National. He's got 11 st. 10 lb. there. He's being ridden by Owen McNally. He's a winner here in soft ground. I think, like Mill House, he'd probably be happier if there was more give in the going. The ground is *very* fast here today. Caduval, a ten-year-old, the oldest member of the party. Mill House and Arkle both eight-year-olds and Stoney Crossing a seven-year-old. In point of fact, Stoney Crossing having been foaled in Australia, will be little more than six because they have a different foaling time there – Southern Hemisphere time – so Stoney Crossing will be only six-and-a-half.

'And there we have Owen McNally, the rider of Caduval, with Mrs. Owen and Toby Balding. Who will make the running here? It'll be quite a difficult problem for the jockeys involved, especially those of Mill House and Arkle. But Arkle's shown Pat Taaffe that he can go along in front or come from behind and win. That's why he appeals to us so greatly as a *real* champion.

'And there's Willie Robinson, Bill Gollings on the left and Fulke Walwyn, the official giving the signal to mount, and Willie perhaps in a more fortunate position than Pat, less nerve-wracking anyway.

'Stoney Crossing the only one of the four which has not yet been mounted . . . Bill Roycroft was looking at one of Stoney Crossing's forelegs as if there might have been something wrong with the horse's shoeing, but all seems to be well now. He's in the green and gold colours of Australia. He's a rather plain-looking horse who's going to have a very unusual experience. He's got a good old saddle on him, this horse. It's not a typical racing saddle by any means . . . I think we'll find he's got a very different style, this Australian, to the professional steeplechase jockeys. He rides considerably longer in the leg. He hasn't got his toes in the stirrups yet. But a very notable horseman from a great horse country, and now he's taking up his proper position in numerical order with Mill House leading from Caduval . . .'

Out on the course now and Peter O'Sullevan takes over:

'They've got quite a little way to jog back to the three miles, two furlongs and seventy-six yards start for the fortieth running of the Cheltenham Gold Cup, run over twenty-one fences . . .

'Mill House looking eager to get on with the job – to have a crack at regaining the title he won in 1963. Arkle also very keen, just pulled up in the corner there. He can take a pretty strong hold, this horse.

'The going must be just about perfect in contrast to the first day and to some extent yesterday. We haven't seen horses slipping up, sliding on the ground, which certainly was *greasy* on the first day. These are perfect conditions for steeplechasing, beautiful clear light, the sun shining and an immense crowd attracted by the prospect of seeing these two notable steeplechasers in action.

'They're under starter's orders.

'They're off! Arkle and Mill House together at the first, Mill House on the far side. Side by side. Caduval jumps it third and Stoney Crossing fourth.

'Coming up to the second, stride for stride. Arkle on the near side, Mill House on the far side, stride for stride over it. And Caduval had a *long* look at it. Stoney Crossing jumped it well. And now a long run to the next fence as they cross onto the new course here at Cheltenham, going at a steady pace, Arkle ears pricked just the leader from Mill House.

'Running down to the third with Arkle just the leader from

Mill House. Very nice, neat jump there by Stoney Crossing in third place. This is the water, number 4: Arkle from Mill House.

'This is an open ditch. Arkle from Mill House, Stoney Crossing – and Caduval's some way behind the other three with Stoney Crossing remaining quite well in touch – beautiful jump by Stoney Crossing in third place there! Real exhibition stuff by these star horses, Arkle and Mill House, and Stoney Crossing certainly not being disgraced by them at all at the moment. Arkle running down the hill a good four lengths clear now of Mill House, who's six lengths clear of Stoney Crossing. All coasting at the moment.

'Coming to the next . . . Mill House went a little bit through the top there!

'Bill Roycroft on Stoney Crossing is looking to have a real good chance of the £1,089 third prize here. Arkle, the leader by a length and a half from Mill House. They come to the next. Arkle and – Mill House just put in a little quick one and got almost with him as he got to it. This is the water: number 14. Arkle the leader almost a fence in front of Caduval now. Arkle from Mill House – and Mill House a *bad* one there! That's the first real error that either of these two horses have made. Mill House *trying* to keep in touch with this incomparable champion. Arkle over from Mill House. And Mill House a nice jump there! He drew quite a cry of admiration from the crowd in the stands there, as he got within reach of Arkle at that one.

'Arkle and Mill House . . . and Mill House another good jump – right upsides, Stoney Crossing about ten lengths behind him and Caduval a long, long way behind, a long way behind. Now running down the hill and the race begins really in earnest and very little in it between the two now.

'And Mill House a *mistake* there! He tried to measure that one, stride for stride with Arkle, and Arkle *very* nearly had him on the floor there!

'. . . Mill House almost up with him again. And now racing

for the home turn. And it's still Arkle the leader from Mill House. Mill House under pressure now. Willie Robinson asking him for everything, and it doesn't look as though he's going to get Arkle off the bit, as they round the home turn now with Pat Taaffe looking over his right shoulder, Mill House trying to make ground on his inner. Stoney Crossing is in third place. Caduval is a fence behind them almost.

'And now Arkle opening up now, like a sports car, like a real – as though he's just changed gear! He's opened up, he's changed up, and he's come into the last fence full of running. He's just going to jump it. And a *brilliant* jump! A *superb* jump at the last! Exhibition stuff!

'A fine effort by Mill House but he's absolutely unavailing against the champion. He *is* the greatest, going away to the line, Pat Taaffe riding him out, the horse really enjoying himself. He's given a great exhibition performance this afternoon. This is his second successive Gold Cup. Here's the former Gold Cup winner of 1963, Mill House just passing the post . . . And a great cheer from the crowd for Bill Roycroft on Stoney Crossing as he comes up to qualify for the £1,089 10s. third prize . . . Caduval *very* tired, just jumping the last fence now.

'There's Pat Taaffe looking back over his shoulder to see Caduval now only halfway between the last fence and the winning line. The official result of the 1965 Fortieth Running of the Cheltenham Gold Cup is First, Number Six, Arkle, owned by the Duchess of Westminster, trained in Ireland by Tom Dreaper and ridden by Pat Taaffe. Second, Number Two, Mill House, owned by Mr. Bill Gollings, trained by Fulke Walwyn, ridden by Willie Robinson. Third, Number Five, Stoney Crossing, owned by Mr. Bill Roycroft, trained by him and ridden by him, and fourth of the four runners, Number Four, Caduval, owned by Mrs. Arthur Owen, trained by Toby Balding, ridden by Owen McNally. The distance, twenty lengths and thirty lengths.'

'Better than ever and certainly improved since last year,' said Pat Taaffe as he got off, and he smiled about Arkle's prodigiously flamboyant leap, feet over the top of the last fence. It had looked very swanky.

The Duchess was speechless to start with, then she kept repeating 'What an *incredible* engine there must be inside that frame.'

Tom Dreaper said: 'Haven't I won the Irish National for the last five years in succession? Why wouldn't this horse make it six?' And pressed for other plans, suggested 'The Duchess could ride him in The Newmarket Town Plate!'

Willie Robinson made no excuses: 'Arkle's just a sight better horse,' and Mr. Bill Gollings said sadly, for it was coming to be a habit, 'We can't win all the time.'

The champion Flat trainer Paddy Prendergast said: 'That horse would win any English Cesarewitch under top weight!'

His victory broke the all-time British record for a 'chaser. He had now won £36,818.

Surely he'd proved himself now the greatest 'chaser ever? That veteran racing journalist Norman Pegg didn't think so:

'Let's face the facts . . . Golden Miller won five Gold Cups on the trot against Arkle's two,' said Pegg.

'You can't compare Golden Miller's winnings. Prize money in his day was less than 50% of what it is today . . .

'Golden Miller's age when winning his five Gold Cups ranged from five to nine. Arkle's have been seven and eight . . .

'So he'll need to win as an 11-year-old if he is to equal the Miller with five Gold Cups . . .

'I saw Golden Miller win all his big races . . . and I've seen Arkle do likewise . . . and this is my assessment of their merits:

'Arkle is a better fencer but Golden Miller was the cleverer jumper. He could extricate himself from almost any sort of difficulty.

'Arkle measures his obstacles when he's about to jump . . . but Golden Miller skimmed his like a hurdler.

'Arkle may win himself a higher pedestal than The Miller . . . but he has a long way to go.'

But by now most other experienced experts believed in Arkle's unique supremacy.

Arkle did not after all run in the Irish Grand National although its prize had been put up to £4,235 10s. and was obviously his on a silver dish. On the sensible training principle of spreading the goodies round a bit, Tom Dreaper sent Mr. Craigie's Splash off instead to win this little bout with Paddy Woods in the saddle.

Himself waited five more days to return to England for the £8,230 Whitbread Gold Cup over 3 miles 5 furlongs 18 yards at Sandown on Saturday, April 24th. This would be his first race in England outside Cheltenham and Newbury. Naturally he crowned the handicap with 12 st. 7 lb. and everything else in the race now knelt at the bottom with 9 st. 7 lb. excluding their penalties and overweights.

Mill House, who had suffered so doggedly in this race against Dormant in 1964, was no longer in this field, but going out into the green ones. No horse more deserved the attentions of Doctor Greengrass and Doctor Sunshine.

Of only six opponents the two most likely to be placed were Rough Tweed (Larry Major) and Brasher (Jimmy Fitzgerald) 10 st. with his penalty for winning the 3 mile 7 furlongs £3,444 Scottish Grand National a fortnight earlier.

These two started 5 to 1 and 8 to 1 respectively to Arkle's 9 to 4 on. One of the outsiders was Willow King, half-owned by the Duchess of Westminster, formerly, of course, with Tom Dreaper, and now trained by that cheerful, charming Midlands farmer Derek Ancil, who had succeeded to Ronnie Horton's most successful place at Middleton Stoney.

More significant than Arkle's opposition was the gigantic crowd he drew. There *were* other races at Sandown that day, five flat affairs and possibly quite good ones, too, but the crowd came milling in to see himself.

The Times reported:

'Saturday must have been Sandown Park's most profitable card for a long time. Arkle was the cause. Great horses are the answer to a racecourse manager's prayer, and the lack of them has been one of the chief reasons for disappointing attendances in the past ten years. If anyone believed that the people of this country in a mechanized age had lost their love of a good horse, he would have had his answer in the cheers that began as Arkle crossed the final fence and only ended when he walked jauntily from the winner's enclosure back to his stable.'

Again Arkle felt too full of himself to settle, but sticking his neck out, dashed off towards the first fence, bounded ridiculously high over it, and set out to show that he could lead all the way with 12 st. 7 lb. over 3 mile 5 furlongs if that made it harder for him and easier for the others.

Skipping along like this down the hill on the left, over the third, round the right-hand bend, into the fourth, the first on the railway-stretch and then, right outside the wings, miles off, he sprang at the fence, so far off he could not make it and wallop! He gave it such a belting that the great crowd yelped as if it had been punched in its corporate belly. When we unblinked our eyes there was Arkle cruising along and Pat Taaffe with the short, short stirrup-leathers sitting as still as if his knees were pinioned together (they meet above the withers) and as if his feet were bolted into Arkle's girth.

He never looked like making another mistake and continued to lead pursued by Brasher till they came to the water the last time. Here Brasher headed him, but Arkle went on again at the last fence on the far side and without regard for the extra $2\frac{1}{2}$ stone which now, after three swift miles, should surely be steadying him, darted ahead by three lengths. Going to the last Jimmy Fitzgerald booted Brasher up to Arkle's quarters, but then Pat pressed another magic button and another further squirt of acceleration landed Arkle up the hill.

He won by five lengths, with Willow King (Stan Mellor) loping along twenty lengths behind Brasher in third place. Rough Tweed, another four lengths back, was fourth. The time, 7 minutes 31.8 seconds, was 15.2 seconds under average.

The cheering had broken out like banners all along the stands as he came towards the last fence and it followed him up like thunder as he went past the post. Then occurred a minor riot, as thousands of otherwise sensible people, began to shove, elbow, fight their way like a mob down off the stands and up the hill at a rumble and down the slope in a great cheering, clapping, shouting, wave to fill the amphitheatre round the unsaddling enclosure.

Tom Dreaper thought he had taken off so far back at that 4th fence that he might even land before he got to it. Pat Taaffe reported that, when clear in front and interested in his new surroundings, Arkle had thought of turning rather sharper right up the 5 furlong flat course which at that point intersects the jumping circuit.

Another season ended and he went back to Ireland to go for his holiday. Whether the going at Sandown was a little firmer than expected, or whether he struck that 4th fence very hard indeed is not known, but he did have a noticeable amount of heat in his off-fore fetlock joint on his return to Kilsallaghan. He had evidently jarred it and it was given a mild blister to disperse the inflammation while he was turned out at Bryans-town, Maynooth. In fact, the blister worked more briskly than expected and took quite a hold, and this may well have been a blessing, for the joint so far has caused no trouble.

Eleven

ARKLE WAS invited to the Royal Dublin Society's Show at Ballsbridge to be exhibited, a performance which gives him and his fans equal pleasure: he from the receiving of hot waves of adulation; they from another opportunity to ogle.

It had been planned that Pat Taaffe would ride him over a few exhibition jumps in the middle of that most beautiful flower- and privet-ringed showground. But his veterinary surgeon, Maxie Cosgrove, advised caution: jumping on the joint so soon after the inflammation caused by the blister would mean that further jarring could stir trouble. So, instead, Arkle just walked and trotted round, but did this with such style and flamboyance that he seemed to be taking off the show hacks and hunters who usually extend themselves there before several thousand judging eyes.

Pat Taaffe recalls from those days of parades an amusing example of Arkle's intelligence. When going racing the horse, of course, motors, flies, motors, flies, boxing-up, unboxing as if he were born to travel. Nothing perturbs him at all, as we've heard from Paddy Woods and Liam McLoughlin.

Now to get him to his show parades at Ballsbridge he was first boxed from home to the Sales Paddocks, where he rested like an actor before a personal appearance, and was then re-boxed to get him across the main road and into the showground. 'Couldn't he have walked?' I asked. Pat said, 'He'd have been mobbed, do you see!' I imagined the scene as thousands of showgoers smart, scruffy, sober, drunk suddenly realised that 'himself' were among them: what a chance to tweak hairs from his tail . . . 'C'mon fellahs . . . !'

Arkle submitted gracefully to these motoring operations, these unloadings and stablings and loadings-up again. But only for the first few times. 'Then,' says Pat, 'he refused flatly to get into the horse-box – the only time he ever has!' He was fed up with the preparations for parading and he knew that this wasn't racing. 'How did he know that, d'you think?' asks Pat, 'He's intelligent all right.'

Disappointingly for the gossip columnist few other tales exist to illustrate the wisdom, wit, warmth – even the humanity – of Arkle. He is, sadly for the sentimentalists, too great a horse ever to ape the dreary human. Like a successful sportsman, states-man, or industrialist, he concentrates properly on the job. He has a career to complete, he is responsible to a vast public, he has to employ Mrs. Betty Dreaper practically full time answer-ing his fan mail. He has little time for the baubles and fripperies of life.

Betty Dreaper does, however, like the way he found her daughter's tennis ball. Valerie, then aged eight, was bouncing the ball in the Yard outside Arkle's box (for a disturbance one tenth of this Newmarket and Epsom lads have been garotted) and of course the thing flies over Arkle's half-door and into the straw. So in pops Valerie and scuffles about the price-less wonder horse and fails to find the ball. As she's coming out, a shade disconsolate, she gets a nudge in the back from Arkle's nose, looks round and up, and there's the ball held in the horse's teeth and craftily presented.

Mrs. Beatrix Potter did a lot more with her animals and everyone knows they're true. But what this incident shows me is the friendliness with which Arkle is treated, and the equal, thoughtful courtesy which he so helpfully reciprocates. He might *play* tennis, too, if it didn't interfere with his career . . .

Pat Taaffe's debt and loyalty to Tom Dreaper are already known. He has a singular reverence for the elderly trainer of Kilsallaghan for whom he has worked since 1950: an abnormal-ly long partnership in a profession as full of break-ups as marriages in the entertainment business – but for different reasons. Trainers who are slipping can sometimes steal themselves a bit more rope, a respite from their owners' wrath, by sacking the stable jockey. Prime Ministers, however, seemingly unflappable, have done the same with ministers.

In England one of the longest and most loyal partnerships in jumping was that between Ryan Price and Fred Winter. Price backed Winter through his early falls and failures. The debt of trust was paid back happily and in full. Pat Taaffe, too, has come to an eminence through the usual painful accidents and injuries which grapple every professional jockey down. It has been a long, horsey, friendly, family road since the August of 1940 when he rode 'Daddy's pony Magnolia' at the age of ten in a children's jumping competition at the Dublin Horse Show where Arkle – twenty-five years later – was parading. It was Pat's first jump in a big public horse show and he won the second rosette and a hunting crop from the American Ambassador for the best child rider. Some judge had long sight.

In that year Arkle's granddam, Greenogue Princess, arrived at Malahow. In the year of Pat's birth, young Tom Dreaper had arrived at Kilsallaghan.

Taaffe's had his serious injuries: a broken leg almost as soon as he turned professional and joined Tom Dreaper, which knocked him out of the ring for two fretful months, costing him the rides on Shagreen and Stormhead in the English and Irish Nationals. Six years later in 1956 he suffered a monstrous fall, at little Kilbeggan in the summer, which cracked his skull so badly that his career was feared to have ended. But when November came round Dreaper had fancied runners over at Manchester in the two big 'chases which then filled the November Handicap Meeting and now exist only as ghosts below the housing. Pat had been riding out at home and had mended almost miraculously fast. These two important rides at Manchester were to be his first since the crashing fall. Pat, who is still as modest as a new young lad at a big school, suggested to Dreaper that he might not be able to do them justice. Dreaper was firm. Both won.

Down the gilt lists of great horses he's ridden were the dams of both the two rivals of this story, Arkle and Mill House.

'Funny,' he says, in the large dining-room of the grey block farmhouse on his land at Alasty, near Straffan in Co. Kildare, 'both were only two mile mares. And Mill House's dam – Nas na Riogh – she fell a good deal.'

He farms 125 acres now: 'a few cattle and sheep and I do a bit of tillage. And what I *hope* to do, eventually, is to start a little stud.'

He does not believe, as the clock, another trophy, booms like Big Ben, and the tape-recorder hums and some of his children pop in and out, and we drink coffee and flap the pages of form books and stud books, that *any* distance is too far for Arkle, under any conditions. 'Four-and-a-half miles, say, at Sandown?' 'Oh, I'd say he'd stay that'. I wondered if he would like to ride him at Liverpool. 'I would, yeh – but the Duchess – she doesn't want to risk him. He'd jump round it quite easily, but it's the loose horses – they cause more trouble in the National than anything. And you'd have to settle him in the middle and there – with the loose horses – you'd chance your luck.'

Talking in February, 1966, Pat reckoned 'I get the feeling he'd never fall, he's too clever. But he may fall I suppose through over-confidence.' And, of course, through inattention at Cheltenham the next month, he cast the fence a hefty clout.

I wondered whether anything in the *feel* of Arkle reminded Pat of other horses he had ridden. Generally a jockey can liken aspects of one horse to things that he remembers of another and this is a shorthand communication between jockey and trainer: 'The way he jumps would be like old Fried Egg . . . now when he's tired he hangs just like old Bacon did . . .' and so on. A similitude always exists somewhere. Pat thought for a very long time while the clock ticked and the tape hummed. 'No. He's unequal to any horse. The feel he gives you is quite different. Even when he's *walking* – with his head held up there, y'know.'

'It looks very uncomfortable.'

'No. When you start to canter him, don't take hold of his head.' Let his head be, and he'll put it down – a terrific horse to ride that way. I've *never* found him doing anything wrong – bucking, whipping round, anything like that.'

Where others would pluck the blooms of credit for the victories of a famous partnership, Pat freely discards all. He declares that the different tactics in each race are all dictated by Arkle himself. 'If the pace is strong, he'll settle well enough till he feels it's time to go on. But if they go too slow at the start, he'll go on then and make his own running! As you've seen!'

I wondered if Pat rode him into the fences in any special way.

'No. I just let him alone. I never give him a kick at all now – a squeeze maybe, but not even that near the start of a race. Otherwise he'd take off too early.'

I asked him about schooling.

'He schools over fences at home on his own, now – straight down. As Mr. Dreaper says "There's no use trying to get anything to go along with him!" But on a racecourse he does school with Flyingbolt'.

Every autumn Arkle schools round fences on a racecourse at least twice, and like all Dreaper's horses, he jumps the fences again two or three days before each race he runs. There are six big fences at home, but in the winter they don't jump numbers 5 or 6, leaving these from being cut up for summer use. All six are the same height as racecourse fences, 'but the bars are lower,' says Pat. 'And the third one's over a ditch, and the sixth you jump out of one high field into a low field – quite a drop!'

I supposed that one day Arkle and Flyingbolt would have to meet. 'It'll be a terrible day for me' said Pat. 'I couldn't ride both and one would have to be beaten. If they did happen to meet, *in a match*, Arkle would trot up. But in a race, with six or seven runners it *might* be different. I don't know.'

He meant that a reasonably sized field would ensure a fair, strong pace throughout – the gallop that prevents any sprinter from pouncing on any plodder at the end of a false run race. Pat continued to reflect, weighing the remembered feel of both horses on the run-in. He added, 'I think Arkle would *always* beat him for that extra speed at the end. I feel he's always got some acceleration left, whereas Flyingbolt – if something came at him very quick on the run-in . . .' His voice trailed in doubt.

I wondered how far Flyingbolt would stay. 'At the moment, three miles. I wouldn't like to see him now at three miles and five furlongs, but then he's only seven.'

Arkle's race which has given Taaffe most pleasure so far is 'that first Gold Cup! The tension was terrific. That was *the* terrific thrill.' Faith, tinged with doubt, tested and proved is always a triumph. Afterwards the victories became expected. Some of the tingle was lost. He feels Arkle would win on any course, twisty and hilly as Tramore, flat as Doncaster, on ground from heavy to firm. 'He doesn't mind the firm now, anymore.' And the horse has no preference for right or left-hand tracks.

In 1955 Pat married Molly Lyons; they have five children, and they have lived at Alasty ever since their marriage. The rooms are full of cups and pictures of horses and children popping in, and piping and going lingeringly out. Molly Taaffe brings soup and bread. 'Sure you'll get nothing on the way to Ballymacoll.' She gives you quite a stern look at first meeting, but she's kindness in person in a land where most persons are very kind indeed by English standards.

Molly's very keen on racing and goes a lot. 'Is she frightened?'

'What? No. No. But if I have a fall I get up as soon as I can to show her . . .'

The children go along, too, to the local meetings when they're on holiday, like Fairyhouse and Punchestown. 'Not when there's a great crowd though: they might get lost in it. They don't ride much. They're not that keen. They had an old pony and one day they'd all want to ride and then perhaps none of them for weeks!'

He would quite like one boy to ride. 'But it depends if he'd like it. It's unfair to push him. But if he likes it – let him. Whatever he wishes to do, really . . .'

Very tall for a jockey at nearly six feet, he is slim, with the look of a first-class golfer about him (he isn't). He has far more swing and grace in his frame than is usual in thick-shouldered, often squat jockeys. His weight can still be got down to 10 st.

148

5 lb. He has a pink boyish face, very pale hair, and is so deferential – 'wouldn't you think?' 'You'd know about that . . .' and so on, that one's instinct is to feel he is pulling your leg. He adores his parents, now both very elderly, calls them Daddy and Mummy, and is pleased that brother 'Tos' is with them, carrying on the training stables so well.

Horses he rode years ago canter quickly back into his mind, and he speaks their names with real affection. I told him a decent mare I'd bought from his father was now back in Ireland at stud. 'Gallery Goddess? She won at Cheltenham for you . . . yes. I'll go down and see her. I'd like to see her again.'

He waves from the door, grinning, 'See you at Cheltenham, then, please God.'

He has about him, but in a gentler manner, the *goodness* so remarkable in Fred Winter. Both would be singularly embarrassed by the quality and pinkly deny it – proof that it exists. Being with either makes one feel better: less mean; more charitable, more hopeful about human nature. I find the same in Sir Gordon Richards, a former champion jockey under the other rules, who is so obviously, even on first meeting, 'a really *decent* man.' Some sharp hot jockeys have certainly done well, but none, I think, has ever been a champion. Can there, in this field, at least, exist a link between goodness and success?

Twelve

THE SEASON of 1965/66 began for Arkle without his customary paid exercise round Gowran Park, and his first race wasn't till November 6th at Sandown, a week or so later than usual. The race selected was nominally a new one: the £5,165 Gallaher Gold Cup, the natural successor (if an offspring can beget it's Dad) of that firm's Senior Service Trophy of exactly that value at the same meeting in 1964. The distance now was 3 miles 118 yards instead of 3 miles 125 yards in the previous year when Dreaper's Fort Leney (Pat Taaffe) had been a 11/10 favourite and 'ran and jumped stinking' on the firm ground to finish an uneasy fifth.

Arkle's old rival, Mill House, was coming back for another crack and was a runner now. He had already two races stashed under his deep girth. First he had churned round Ascot's new jumping circuit in a 2 mile condition race – far too short for him, but an excellent 'opener' – and had run really well to be second to England's star 2 miler Dunkirk. Then Fulke Walwyn had found for him a gift condition race at the previous Sandown meeting, in which for £426 he had had to give only 10 lb. to a poor old horse called Crobeg, whom eight years before I'd tried to buy: luckily for my owner I failed to negotiate a price!

Mill House (Willie Robinson) made all the running to win the match by thirty lengths and yet in 6.5 seconds under average. This was exactly what Mill House's doctors and psychiatrists had ordered.

He, therefore, returned to Sandown full of good cheer, fit and confident: the three prerequisites of any 'chaser, or of any successful man. He was carrying only 11 st. 5 lb. to Arkle's 12 st. 7 lb., handicapper Mr. George Smith thus putting him 16 lb. behind. In the absence of the injured Willie Robinson, Mill House was ridden by one of the best horsemen and most intelligent of professional jockeys 'Frenchie' Nicholson's tall son David. Bar Rondetto 10 st. 9 lb. (Jeff King), Arkle's other opponents in a field of seven were given the 10 stone minimum. (Weights extend to 9 st. 7 lb. only when steeplechases are 3½ miles or longer).

They comprised The Queen Mother's decent old 'chaser The Rip, sired by another horse of hers, Manicou, out of a mare called Easy Virtue by Scottish Union. The Rip, now dashingly named, was formerly called Spoilt Union and was the winner over six seasons and despite various troubles, of two hurdle races, and twelve 'chases from the super-efficient establishment of Peter Cazalet at Fairlawne, Kent. He had been placed in his two previous runs at Kempton and Ascot and was obviously fit. Recognition of this, stimulated by the racing public's hot affection for his marvellous owner, brought his price in from 33's to 20's. A bookmaker rashly remarked as he took some sentimental money – 'Know why we stay in business? Mug punters backing horses they'd *like* to win, not horses they think *will*!'

Another great National Hunt supporter, Edward Courage from Edgcote, Warwickshire, had his home-trained Lira in the field. She, too, had run and been placed, but the bookies confidently classed her a 100 to 1 nonsense-runner in a field of seven. There was a trifle of money for Rondetto from 10's to 9's, and John O' Groats (P. Kelleway) winner of twelve races but now first time out this season had the odd supporter at 33 to 1. A ten-year-old gelding called Candy, winner of eight steeplechases in slightly less exalted company, was summarily dismissed as another ludicrous 100 to 1 shot. Mill House opening at 9 to 4, eased a little to 7 to 2, although he had a busy number of loquacious backers trying to convince themselves by telling you that 'he's now right back to his best at last . . . he's fit too and Arkle's not yet run . . . could *any* horse give Mill House at his best 1 stone 2 lb.? . . . he likes this course too doesn't he . . . ?'

For all that, 'himself' was heartily backed in the market from 7 to 4 on down to 9 to 4 on and several plungers reckoned the outlay of £2,000 to win £1,000 in six minutes round Sandown's fences was a better way of earning a living than investing the stuff with drunk or dreary stockbrokers.

The first astonishment was the outbreak of applause as the runners wound their way down the tan track under the rhododendrons and the bandstand, and this, on a grey November day from a stiff-lipped British crowd, erupted into cheering as Arkle and Mill House came onto the course.

But this itself was not the end of an extraordinary demonstration unequalled even in the memories of racing's grey fossils. For as the race began, almost each leap by Mill House and Arkle – and they were really like Nuryev vaulting – sucked from the packed, sparkling crowd not mere oohs and aahs, but clattering bursts of real applause and jets of real hard cheering.

Candy led to the fourth along the railway, then, as they turned up the hill towards the Pond Fence, Mill House went on leaping like a tiger, getting a great ride from David Nicholson, and stirring in many minds the exciting thought that he might really be now as good as he was when champion. Over the Pond Fence and Arkle pulling like a train now, and swing right over the next two up towards the stands and each time, as the great rivals twang through the air like arrows, the dark crowd above returns a roar of cheering. Now on the level again and passing the post first time and Arkle cannot be held any longer and he is away behind the big Tote board down the hill to the first fence again. Thus Arkle, then Mill House swing right again along the railway line, pinging over the fences in the best dual spectacle of jumping ever goggled and gasped at Sandown. And then, as they rush towards the water-jump, the huge Mill House strides past Arkle and his white-blazed head juts out in front and he is leading the champion now! From the stands a moan whips through the crowd like a gale and a hubbub breaks out and everywhere it's the hissing 's's in 'Mill House . . . Mill House . . .'

Hearts thump, hands quiver, glasses jump, eyes strain, comments bullet out of sides of taut mouths – 'Arkle's beat!' 'No, never!' 'Is, I tell you, look!' 'Pat's not moved.' 'He's kicking on'. 'Watch Mill House then!' 'Watch Arkle, blast you!'

Mill House was now – and with less than mile to go – no less than three lengths clear of the champion and the crowd was almost mad. Still Mill House led as they started to turn for home and it seemed even that he had increased the gap to four lengths. Some cried out 'Arkle! Come on Arkle!' And the punters squealed like tortured slaves: 'Pat! Pat! *Pat!*' And the Mill House fan club loosed its old great roar, for here was the old hero, the great horse from England getting at last his sweet revenge on Arkle.

Then, in a ridiculous instant, all was done. At that stage of a thundering race the gap between the two vanished in a dozen strides. Literally in twelve swinging strides Arkle shot up to Mill House and caught him like a monitor catching a naughty boy. And on the bend for the Pond Fence away he came. From that moment and home over the last two fences a greater roar than any ever heard on any British racecourse surged like a typhoon over Sandown.

When Arkle twitched the lead in a twinkle from the all-out Mill House the big horse's spirit cracked. At the Pond Fence he weakened rapidly and Rondetto came past him to follow Arkle home twenty lengths behind. Mill House was third, twenty-four lengths behind Arkle and thus, being already in receipt of 16 lb., could be classified now as 40 lb. behind him. A Gold Cup winner nearly 3 stone inferior to another horse? Impossible! Except with Arkle.

But by the time The Rip – fifteen lengths fourth behind Mill House – had landed over the last fence the crowd had burst in torrents from the stands and was rushing to cheer their hero in.

Arkle was so unaffected by the race that Pat had hardly slipped his saddle off in the enclosure before he was rootling head down through the brown dank autumnal leaves and chewing mouthfuls of them in the belief, Paddy Woods thought, that they might well be chocolate papers.

It then appeared that Arkle had broken the course record. In February Mill House had clocked 6 minutes 16 seconds for the 3 miles 118 yards. Arkle broke this by no less than 17 seconds to return 5 minutes 59 seconds – over half a minute under average time.

It had been a fantastic race.

With his earnings up by £5,165 Arkle flew home to Kilsallaghan. There were three weeks only to his next visit: Newbury again, for another go at the 3¼ mile Hennessy Gold Cup worth this year £7,099 5s.

This time Arkle had a fellow raider: Tom Dreaper sent along Mr. Clifford Nicholson's bright youngster Dicky May to run in the Oxfordshire Chase on the previous day, Friday, November 26th. This, a two mile condition race for five- and six-year-olds was worth £800 10s. and Dicky May odds-on, as now seems fitting for all Dreaper horses on an English visit, won quite comfortably. Lest he might fall and injure Arkle's jockey for the morrow, Dreaper had put Liam McLoughlin up in place of Pat Taaffe.

Mill House was not of the company in the Hennessy. Nor was he, in fact, to run again for another two months. This meant that Arkle had no opponent who seemed capable of inclusion with him in any sort of race and his starting price reflected this ludicrous situation. Here was a handicap worth over £7,000 in which (as theoretically as in communism) all horses had an equal chance of winning, and in which Arkle was lumbered with 12 st. 7 lb., giving 2½ stone, or very near it, to all his seven opponents. Yet he started at 6 to 1 on – the price of a star against a donkey in a two horse sprint on the flat.

Freddie, 10 st. 3 lb. (Pat McCarron) had the next highest weight in the original handicap. Wayward Queen (J. Cook) ran with a 6 lb. penalty at 10 st. 6 lb.; Happy Arthur (G. Milburn) carried 3 lb. overweight at 10 st. 4 lb. Yet Freddie, now 2 st. 4 lb. below Arkle, had carried topweight (11 st. 10 lb.) in the Grand National eight months earlier, had been hot favourite to win, and had only been beaten ¾ length by Jay Trump who carried 5 lb. less. On this basis Arkle's weight in the National should have been 14 stone!

It patently now required a range of at least four stone to allow even a handful of horses any chance with him. The situation had really got out of hand. Never in the world's long history of racing under all rules had one animal so dominated all others that he seemed to be a different being.

No real betting business was done on the race. The gigantic crowd packed in to watch, not punt, and the nimble makers of books introduced special place betting which hardly seemed generous enough to tempt the public: 2 to 1 on Freddie, 5 to 4 on Wayward Queen, 3 to 1 against Brasher (J. Fitzgerald) whom Arkle met on precisely the same terms as in the last 'Whitbread' when he beat him five lengths. It was 3 to 1 against a place for Happy Arthur and John O' Groats (P. Kelleway) . . .

Yet what seemed likely to be merely a triumphant procession – and even fanatics weary of too easy victories too often – produced in fact a ding-dong battle between Arkle and Brasher, a self-admitted tactical error by Pat Taaffe, a couple of 'reminders' administered to the mighty horse, and a tired hero on the run-in who for once could find no dazzling flash of foot.

If Brasher, born in 1956, and sold as a youngster when his breeder, Miss Dorothy Paget, died, had only possessed good legs he might well have been the British champion in Arkle's absence. I had led an owner of mine by the nose to bid for him at Ballsbridge when he came up with thirty-two others at Miss Paget's Executors' Sale in April, 1960 – the sale prior to Arkle's. Brasher was bought by Mr. Gosschalk that day for the very reasonable price of 2,500 guineas, for he'd shown promise already. My owner's limit then was 1,500 guineas, though he subsequently aimed rather higher, and in a different, more damaging direction.

Brasher turned out a good buy: he won two good hurdle races and was placed twice from his first season of six races, and won again next season from only two starts. Then trouble plagued his legs and in the next two seasons he could run only five times. But in 1964/65 trainer Tommy Robson of Penrith had a marvellous season with him for Mr. Gosschalk winning the £3,444 Scottish Grand National (at the last meeting to be held at Bogside), and the £930 Grand National Trial at Catterick, before running second to Arkle in the Whitbread Gold Cup.

This season, trained by Pat Taylor in Robson's enforced absence, he had had an outing at Wetherby on November 6th, in which he had clouted his jockey off when lying last, before coming to Newbury to run the finest race of his career and possibly, and sadly, the last.

The ground, officially described as 'good' was in fact of that displeasing holding type to which Newbury's prone: no spring in it, nor any looseness either – very tiring indeed if you have got to drag four feet out of it every blessed stride for 5,802 yards. Being a 'chaser is not all bright oats and Guinness.

Despite this, the nine-year-old Brasher and the thirty-year-old James Gerard Fitzgerald (recreations: tennis and farming) jumped out of the gate like centaurs onto the centre court and away down the back-stretch and under the wood they went, winging along in front over the first four fences.

Arkle pursued. At the fifth, the last fence on the far side, he grabbed the lead off Brasher, but as they swung left-handed towards us, Brasher snatched it back again. There was remarkably little between the two horses, (except a difference of 2½ stone as purists pointed out) and as they jumped several times together Brasher clearly beat the champion through the air; jumping faster, landing further out and getting away from touch-down that fraction quicker. These surprising small supremacies rather peeved both Lord Arkle and Patrick Taaffe, Esquire.

From the open ditch in the straight (where Arkle's slip had lost his first Hennessy) to the open ditch on the far side it was Brasher leading at a really strong gallop in this going. Pat Taaffe kept sending Arkle along with him and at the fence after the far open ditch, the fourteenth, he went ahead again.

At this point – Pat admits frankly now – he made a serious tactical error. 'If Arkle had been beaten that day, it would have been entirely my fault. I was wrong to go on pushing on after I'd passed Brasher. There wasn't any point in it. My horse was out on his own all that way in front. If anything, I was just making the race for Freddie! Don't you think it was quite wrong not to have stayed with Brasher?'

In the heat of a race there is no time for deliberations. Incidents dictate tactics in instants: Pat let Arkle go bowling on ahead alone. Brasher was falling back and so hot was the pace that Freddie with a mile to go was nearly thirty lengths behind him.

Coming to his old bête noire open ditch, No. 19 on his card, Arkle met it wrong, screwed in the air to clear it and landed slightly sideways. A puff of panic in the crowd – then Arkle was coming on. By now Brasher was quite shaken off, but Freddie was observed gradually making up ground.

Two more to jump, one more – and then Arkle suddenly, for the first time in my experience, started to tire. The fizz was gone from his action, he was no longer running freely, and as the crowd on the course began to press in round the last fence he hesitated. Pat's stick smartly slapped his shoulder. 'I don't think he knew where he was meant to jump,' said Pat afterwards. 'He was looking at the people.' And certainly as the crowd squeezed in, Arkle came across to the right and jumped crookedly. (See picture opposite page 96)

He got over the last, but only reasonably, and paused on landing like a tired horse, and he was visibly fatigued on the run-in. Pat sat down to ride him hard for home and gave him another slap, for Freddie had passed Brasher and was now less than twenty lengths behind, and progressing excellently as his $4\frac{1}{2}$ mile stamina began to play. And as Pat says 'If I'd let Arkle dawdle there he might not have got started again.'

All Arkle's supporters were pleased when the post came, with Freddie fifteen lengths behind. The good Brasher was third a total of eighteen lengths behind, an improvement in Arkle's favour of thirteen lengths or nearly another stone on their

Whitbread result eight months before.

Pat said afterwards to me 'Mr. Dreaper and the Duchess didn't say anything, but I knew I'd ridden a bad race.' For the first time since Arkle had started steeplechasing three years before Pat felt that he would have produced no turn of foot if challenged on the run-in.

On a day when the times of all the other races were longer than usual, Arkle's 6 minutes 49.2 seconds for the course was 5.8 seconds under average. His total earnings now exceeded £56,000.

So far this season the Irish at home had not seen their hero in action, and they were still to be deprived of him. His next race was to be the King George VI steeplechase at Kempton Park on Boxing Day. This, a condition race not a handicap, has become one of jumping's few semi-classics since its inception in 1951. It has been won by Cheltenham Gold Cup winners like Limber Hill (1955), Mandarin (1957 and 1959) Saffron Tartan (1960) and Mill House (1963). It has been won, too, by excellent horses who just failed to gain 'chasing's crown (as Tom Dreaper says 'I'd rather win one Gold Cup than four Grand National handicaps!') – horses like Halloween (1952 and 1954) and Lochroe (1958). Kempton's a peculiar track, – Arkle had never seen it before – very flat, very fast, rather sharp and on the turn, and takes very little staying: a top two miler, Peter Cazalet's Rose Park won the King George VI in 1956 and my crack two miler Flame Gun ran very well in it in 1959. It takes, however, a great deal of jumping: the fences are the next stiffest after Aintree.

Though not quite a level weight classic like the Gold Cup, the King George VI's conditions permit a star of Arkle's power to run at levels with only reasonably good winners, and to give away under a stone to novices. The race thus fitted Arkle like a golden glove. All opposition retreated in a rout and fears rose that the champion would walk over for £5,000. This whisper attracted those with an eye for the excellent place money, and it also encouraged that grand supporter of 'chasing, Colonel Billy Whitbread, and his trainer Peter Cazalet to risk their brilliant two mile 'chaser Dunkirk (Bill Rees) to ensure that Arkle got a gallop and the public got a race.

It is to Colonel Whitbread's lasting credit in the history of steeplechasing that by his example and the generosity of his companies he launched the new wave of sponsored races. Sponsorship is a blood transfusion, not a cure for racing's financial anaemia, but without it racing's outer limbs were already dying. Whitbread started the rescue service.

Dormant (Stan Mellor), who had beaten Mill House for the Whitbread when trained by forthright Captain Neville Crump, was alleged to have had several dozen trainers since then and to have spent more time in horse boxes on the move than in any stable. He was a runner, we understood from his past and present trainers, and he, like Dunkirk, carried the same weight as Arkle: 12 st. The only other competitor was the novice Arctic Ocean, who carried 11 st. 3 lb. including R. Walker, a claiming jockey ineligible for his allowance due to the high value of the contest.

Snaigow and Rondetto, who might have run, sensibly did not. The pundits had little summing up to do for what seemed a certain comfy hack round and several turned to the Arkle-Golden Miller argument.

Clive Graham of the *Daily Express*, a kind and deceptively sleepy looking expert, knows very nearly the lot. 'I come down categorically in favour of Arkle,' he declared, making the excellent point that Golden Miller had had several close level-weight tussles in his life, particularly with Thomond II, whereas Arkle dominated the opposition even in handicaps. 'To my mind,' said Clive Graham, 'Arkle is the most amazing steeplechaser we have ever seen.' He was sure he would win a Cambridgeshire over nine furlongs, and recalled with amazement that the trainer of Arkle's sire, the 400 guinea reject Archive, had said of him 'he had a heart no bigger than that of a mouse.'

The ground on Boxing Day, Monday, December 27th, 1965, was officially called 'good'. It was in fact firm and frosty and racing was in doubt. Huntingdon, Market Rasen, Sedgefield,

Wincanton, Wetherby and Wolverhampton were all frosted off.

Tom Dreaper was in bed with 'flu back at Greenogue, and Arkle was in the charge of Johnny Lumley and a new small work rider, because Liam McLoughlin and Paddy Woods were both wanted to ride Dreaper horses at Leopardstown. He had arrived several days earlier at the racecourse stables. It was here, as he was being saddled for his morning pipe-opener, that the stabling manager looked into his box and saw to his astonishment Arkle 'crouching down to let the small lad climb up on him!' Heroes trail clouds of gossip in their wake and soon it was being said on the course that Arkle was saddling himself up. In fact, as we already know, he was merely giving his daily saddling stretch-and-yawn. Sensible in itself: it lets the girths fit snugly.

Was the frosty ground likely to be dangerous? The Duchess and Betty Dreaper conferred.

The Duchess declared that even if the ground was treacherous she felt she must allow Arkle to run because of all the thousands who had turned out to see him, and of all the millions squatting pregnant with hope and Xmas pud before their goggling telly sets.

The promise of his appearance lured extra thousands out. The roads were jammed with Arkle pilgrims, an hour's run took three, and car parks crammed to bursting point were closed. Kempton chairman Henry Hyde said comfortably 'It's just like the old times.'

And indeed it was the biggest crowd at Kempton on a Boxing Day since the dear boom days for entertainment back in 1954. Fears nagged about the going. Frost still glittered greyly. Breaths hung in the cold air and in this midwinter the first race was as early as 12.30. This was preceded by a touch of the necessary showman – a parade of old champions. Pacing or jiggling, sleek and rugged, or wild and woolly, some of the kings who had once stood on Arkle's throne proceeded round the paddock and past the stands. The need for homage and warm hands produced an ovation, as two Grand National winners, Kilmore and the grey Nicolaus Silver, and three

Cheltenham Gold Cup winners, Mandarin, Pas Seul and Saffron Tartan, and two previous winners of this King George VI Steeplechase, Manicou and Halloween, were included in a sort of equine British Legion parade.

There is little to say about the race so far as Arkle is concerned: the sun of his easiest victory yet, and at 7 to 1 on, was thickly clouded by the sadness over Dunkirk and Bill Rees. The two mile crack, who always bowled along in front, cutting his opponents down, again attempted these tactics against the staying champion. He set a scorching pace, and was so far clear entering the straight for the first time that the crowd wondered if Taaffe was not being oversure of Arkle and might not this be a Cazalet repeat of the Rose Park turn-up?

By the time they passed the winning post for the first time Arkle, without appearing to surge forward, had quietly contracted the gap to twenty lengths, and continued its steady reduction as they swung away from us right-handed and over the water. As they turned right again at the far bend the gap was eight lengths and Dunkirk had covered two miles, the limit of his stamina. He jumped the first fence on the far side a weakening horse and Arkle was only three lengths behind.

Pat Taaffe, seeing Dunkirk jump it so badly, feared he might fall at the next and possibly fetch Arkle down. So he immediately squeezed his accelerators and shot Arkle up to, level with, past Dunkirk in a flash as they came in to the next. As Arkle rose, Dunkirk staggered as he reached it, crashed through it and down, turned over on his nearside and died, choking. Bill Rees had half a ton of horse crashing onto him. His right thigh broke and in extreme pain he was still pinned under the dead horse. Six spectators ran to the scene, putting human life much higher than equine glory, and began to tug and pull at Dunkirk's head and tail to try to drag his body off the wretched Rees. Two other spectators bent down between the horse's front and hind legs and taking hold of Rees's arms and shoulders began to haul him out over the scored frosty ground, from under Dunkirk's warm belly.

He was remarkably lucky not to have broken his neck,

for as Dunkirk came crashing down his body ground all over him.

By the time Rees was freed, Arkle was past the post to 'The Arkle roar' from a crowd which could only guess at death and danger on the far side of the course. He passed the post alone as Dormant was landing over the last fence. When Pat took hold of him to pull him up, he returned the pressure and pulled Pat on round the bend and on past the water jump and past the Rank cameramen who were shooting my Look at Life film '*Over the Sticks*', as if he were starting on a third circuit and a fourth mile, tearing away at the *end* of three miles.

The cameras followed up into the unsaddling enclosure where he was made much of by the Duchess and Betty Dreaper and greeted by the crowd. He had now earned another £4,634 to bring his winnings to £61,811 and in the next hour in Ireland Tom Dreaper's Crown Prince (Liam McLoughlin) and Splash (Paddy Woods) won the two biggest races at Leopardstown.

But most of us were at least half thinking about Bill Rees almost on the eve of his thirty-second birthday who had been riding in cracking form. He rode no more all season. It was the other side of racing's whirling coin.

Many of us, seeing how Dunkirk had faltered *before* he reached the last fence in his life, wondered if he had broken a leg going in to it. We were almost right in diagnosis. A post mortem showed that the two mile champion's lungs were congested with blood from a haemorrhage and that he had probably been semi-conscious and almost dead as he lurched into the black birch to fall and break his neck.

The death of Dunkirk spawned two sorts of reaction, both unpleasant. On the one hand the old women of racing and the goo-goo-eyed sentimentalists oozed out weird comparisons between the death of a gelding in a horse-race and the deaths of thousands of Europeans in battle round Dunkerque in 1940. The notion of elevating a sad incident in a sport to the level of a world miracle which was so nearly a tragedy, was in itself in appalling taste. But when one of these people suggested that the dead soldiers of Dunkerque were going to be delighted to have

Col. Whitbread's horse along with them, it was difficult not to be sick.

It shows the fascination of racing that it can extract such mania. But this is also its weakness. It keeps little men's eyes so tied to the target that they lose their sense of proportion. Shut up in their tiny world of almost private passion, they forget they are living only in an excellent sport.

The other nasty reaction was from a band who now dubbed Arkle 'The Killer'. With that smear of faint knowledge which is a comic rather than a dangerous thing, they demonstrated that Arkle 'had finished Mill House, then Brasher; now he'd killed Dunkirk!' They did not actually scream for his trial for murder or demand questions in the House, but they were tediously noisy in some sections of the Press – all of which would have made excellent copy for a sick comedian.

They misconstrued an effect as a motive. There is no doubt that running any horse under severe and continued pressure will harm him as surely as flogging cars flat out down motorways. The bigger and faster the car, the less the pressure: it can seldom be running at 100% exertion. The smaller the output the harder the test. When a horse is gallant he will endure the most pressure before cracking, as in the case of Mill House and Brasher, and any physical weakness will thus be stretched to breaking point. Arkle, by his superiority, has hardly ever endured pressure for more than a minute's length so he should continue sound, into a ripe old age. That is the unfairness of life.

The haemorrhage which caused Dunkirk's last blunder cannot be laid at Arkle's door, for Rees's horse was not trying to keep up with Arkle. Its basic cause almost certainly lay in the epidemic of equine 'flu which has secretly damaged so many horses' lungs. This, coupled with his bold headstrong manner of running, brought him down.

The *Sporting Life* of December 31st, 1965, published forty lines of verse from a reader in a 'Front page tribute' surrounded by thick black lines under 'The Death of a Racehorse'. Mr. D. J. McKeown of Feltham, Middlesex reached his apotheosis eight lines before his conclusion, and in stanza seven, declared:

'He does not know that racing is a sport,
That everyone expected he'd be caught;
He's come to win, and he must finish first:
What matter if his lungs are fit to burst?'

And Tom Dreaper received the usual white shoal of letters one of which said:

'Dear Sir,

I should be glad to receive your assurance that Arkle (the wonder horse of the year) will not run under any adverse conditions.

It would be a tragedy to see him end like Dunkirk. I am unable to get about, but I have watched Arkle on TV and I am sure he has done enough without taking any risks.

I would like a photo of him showing his wonderful head. I am enclosing cheque for 10/–.'

Someone else wrote:

'I am a very great admirer of that lovely half-human animal Arkle and would love to come down to talk to him and pat him, but unfortunately I am denied that pleasure as I am crippled with arthritis – I want you to pat him for me and give him a lump of sugar maybe two or perhaps three with my love. Would you be so kind as to let me have a snap of him, I don't care how small, I would love it.

I hope sincerely he will never meet with a serious accident but will die of old age as I am doing.'

It was the end of another year.

Thirteen

ALTHOUGH ARKLE had been entered for Sandown's Mildmay Memorial 'Chase in January (thereby compressing the handicap and ruining the race) he was not seriously intended to run in it, unless Kempton had been called off. It is essential in training to have different alternative *programmes* not just alternative races. Unless a selection of races is suitably spaced out, one lost engagement puts the whole progress out of gear.

With Kempton secured Tom Dreaper decided that Arkle should have one run in Ireland, either at Gowran Park or Leopardstown, to keep him in trim for his return to England and his third Gold Cup.

'The Thyestes' at Gowran on January 27th was a possibility. But Dreaper, who had won it last year with Fort Leney, selected Flyingbolt who had won his last three races, not Arkle to represent Kilsallaghan. Joy to possess one star in a stable; heaven to train two at once! Flyingbolt (Pat Taaffe) had 12 stone and three of Arkle's old pursuers took him on: Height O'Fashion 10 stone, second, beaten a distance; Flying Wild 9 st. 13 lb., third another 25 lengths behind; and Greatrakes, who fell.

The way in which Flyingbolt slaughtered his field in ground so heavy that one fence had to be cut out, and won £1,324 15s. at his ease, revived speculation about his rating with Arkle. Pat Taaffe stayed loyal to the older horse, but something the great flat trainer Paddy Prendergast said to him after the race stuck in his mind: 'Flyingbolt has done far more by seven years old than Arkle did at the same age . . .'

The rain continued to portend a second Flood. Meeting after meeting was abandoned with waterlogged courses and there seemed again some sense in my recommendations for a revised National Hunt calendar: all January and February blank – the off season; race instead June and July. It will come one day, I hope.

Leopardstown, scheduled for February 19th was waterlogged and postponed. And postponed again. And as the days drew on towards Cheltenham it seemed Arkle would miss his race. This could prove serious in any event, but now it was even graver: the wet which fell on the tracks had made Dreaper's gallops virtually unusable. Arkle was getting fat and losing fitness.

Under Irish racing rules meetings can be postponed almost *sine die*, whereas in England all one can hope for is a postponement within the advertised span of a meeting: Thursday's card being run on the Saturday of a three-day programme. This is to avoid clashings in Britain's crammed weeks; in Ireland there's seldom more than one or two meetings a week in the winter. The Leopardstown February meeting finally took place ten days later on Tuesday, March 1st, and it was worth Tom Dreaper's waiting: he and Pat Taaffe produced a treble with Stonehaven, Thorn Gate and Arkle. Mrs. Baker, Arkle's breeder, was there for the first time in her life to see Arkle run in the flesh and not on television. She was a guest of the Leopardstown Club. 'I saw the race in comfort – a great joy to me! But I'm never happy till he's over the last!'

The champion in fact just scraped home by a neck from the little mare Height O'Fashion to whom he was giving the full range of three stone, and he had the hardest race of his life to do so.

The mare, ridden this time by J. P. Sullivan instead of her usual T. F. Lacy, made up ground stealthily over the last two, came with a great run from the last and caught Arkle on the run-in. He had to be ridden flat out by Taaffe to last home and teetered on the ledge of defeat for the first time since

'The Massey-Ferguson' a year and a quarter earlier. Height O'Fashion was fully fit – she had run again between her Thyestes second to Flyingbolt and this race, which was her tenth of the season. She was also ridden with splendid dash and judgment, and some recollected 3½ years back that President's Hurdle at Gowran Park in October, 1962, when she with 12 stone had been set to give 23 lb. to Arkle. Between then and now a reversal of 4 st. 9 lb!

Even more tried to compare her performance against Flyingbolt – received 2 stone beaten a distance, say 40 lengths; with her run now: received 3 stone beaten only a neck . . .

Conjecture rustled: on the figures it seemed Arkle was slipping back, or Flyingbolt was soaring upwards; in any case the gap between the two mighty horses from Greenogue was dwindling, dwindling perhaps to equality. And Flyingbolt had two years in hand . . .

But Pat Taaffe said afterwards: 'Arkle was *terribly* unfit. He hadn't been able to do any work at all on the ground for weeks.' With this in mind Pat had wanted to exert him as little as possible under the heavy weight in the heavy ground. It seemed possible he could cruise home. Arkle was perhaps over-confident and this may be an expanding flaw in his character. Like the rest of us, repeated praise makes for overweening pride. It cannot have occurred to him that day at Leopardstown that *anything* could come along and catch him, let alone Mr. Donohoe's little old mare from way down south.

It is worth noting that three months earlier in heavy ground at Navan in the big £1,000 three mile 'chase little Height O'Fashion had carried 12 stone to victory giving over 2 stone away to six of her eight opponents. This would have put Arkle in the Navan with 15 stone and we are really getting into dreamland.

So indeed it seemed it was in Arkle's next Gold Cup at Cheltenham sixteen days later on Thursday, March 17th. He started for this at the fantastic price of 10 to 1 on in a field of five of which two, though judiciously running for the rich place monies, would have needed a quarter of a mile start to give them any chance of warming up the champion's engine.

Except for Arkle's previous Gold Cup, only three Cheltenham Gold Cup winners since the war have started odds-on: Tom Dreaper's Prince Regent 7 to 4 on in 1940, and Cottage Rake 6 to 4 on in 1949 and 6 to 5 on in 1950.

Even the pre-war giant Golden Miller in his five victories had never started at anything like this price. He had been 13/2 when he beat Inverse four lengths in 1932, 7 to 4 on beating Thomond II ten lengths in 1933, 6 to 5 against when he beat Avenger six lengths in '34. In 1935 he was 2 to 1 on and beat Thomond II again by three-quarters of a length in their historic duel, and in the year of his last victory 1936, he started 21 to 21 on and beat Royal Mail twelve lengths. There was no race in 1937 and in 1938 Golden Miller, favourite at 7 to 4 against, and ridden by 'Frenchie' Nicholson, was beaten two lengths by Morse Code. In his six Gold Cup races he had had three different trainers and five different jockeys.

Since the race began in 1924 worth £685 only four horses have won the classic more than once: Easter Hero 1929 and 1930, Golden Miller (1932, 33, 34, 35, 36), Cottage Rake (1948, 49, 50) and Arkle (1964, 65, 66 . . .)

The 1966 Gold Cup was worth rather more than ten times the value of the 1924 event: £7,674 10s. and as this was, short of war or similar catastrophe, simply another donation from British racing via Arkle to Anne, Duchess of Westminster, interest in his performance centred literally on the distance by which he would win. He had beaten Mill House by twenty lengths in 1965 – which was twice as far as any other post war verdict. Could he, we wondered, make it thirty lengths now? When the possibility of defeat ceases to exist we can only speculate about the magnitude of victory.

Mill House was out of training with leg trouble. After his punishing defeat by Arkle in the Gallaher in November he had had one more race at Cheltenham, where with all conditions loaded in his favour, he had jumped badly and made heavy weather of beating three third class opponents. It seemed he had fallen for ever from the top class. Then a week before the

Gold Cup his leg went. He had run in bandages ever since he came to Fulke Walwyn, a precaution against trouble, but also a public indication that it could occur at any time. To train a huge horse under these conditions to win so many races was yet another, unpublicised, triumph for one of the best trainers of our time. Had Arkle not been born, or had his career not been manipulated by such wise patient hands, Mill House might have had three golden years at the top and had his name up there with 'The Hero', 'The Miller', and 'The Rake'.

The meeting had started well for the raiding Dreapers. Though Crown Prince had blundered away his favourite's chance in the Totalisator Champion Novice Chase on the first day, Arkloin had won the National Hunt Handicap Chase under joint top weight, and Flyingbolt had cantered round to win the Two Mile Champion Chase both ridden by Pat Taaffe: £4,938 to Dreaper's patrons by Tuesday teatime.

On Wednesday, Thorn Gate (Pat Taaffe) could not beat Arctic Sunset. Flyingbolt, turning out for the Champion Hurdle after weeks of rumour about whether Arkle, Flyingbolt or both or neither might or wouldn't or definitely would run for the hurdlers' crown, finished third to Salmon Spray.

On Thursday, over the old course, Arkle was Dreaper's first runner and Taaffe's first ride of the day. Companies of the crowd disregarded the preceding County Hurdle and were soon three deep and snapping cameras round the prelimary parade ring to see himself appear at 3.30 on St. Patrick's Day wearing a sprig of shamrock jauntily in the near-side of his browband. He moved briskly up and down the steep sides of the ring, attended by Johnny Lumley in black suit and brown suede slippers. Arkle had his head up, looking about him, and had his mouth open most of the time displaying a flashy amount of none-too-sparkling teeth. 'Look! 'E's laughin',' said a fat old lady to no one in particular, 'Laughin' *already*,' and she started to chuckle herself.

Paddy Woods, looking dashing in a turned-up-at-the-back sort of Austrian hat, came bustling in with Arkle's saddle and Johnny Lumley backed him into the black saddling stalls at the top of the hill. Betty Dreaper arrived with an attractive sunburnt daughter and then the Duchess in a red, longish, sensible coat under a fur hat. She had a black handbag and black square-heeled shoes which tapped nervously while Paddy Woods was saddling Arkle. She laughed a good deal with Betty Dreaper, leaning and pointing by the side of the stall, and all the time Arkle, huge hooped ears cocked forward and great brown eyes bulging, stared out over the remembered race-course. It was three-and-a-half years since his first run, first win in England here in the Honeybourne Chase.

There was no uniformed security man hovering closely as there'd been at Kempton, and as the County Hurdle ended there was a stampede of people running up from the back of the stands.

But he was already being led down the hill of the preliminary paddock and through the gap into the main parade ring. 'Did ya see him?' demanded a thick blue-suited Irishman of his wife, as they barged through the throng. 'Did ya *see* him?' His eyes bulged. 'Ah,' said she, wedding-smart in floral hat and marvellous accessories and tossing her head, 'Ah, he's not *that* excitin'.'

'He *is* so!' shouted the husband as if the Pope had been insulted by an Orangeman, but the crowd, already as deep and buzzing as round a Roman amphitheatre with some plump Christian virgins on the bill, fortunately swallowed them up. The previous day's attendance had been a record 20,700. This now increased.

Indeed, the crowd by now were not only on every bench, rod, pole and perch, but each others' shoulders too and clinging like apes up the frames of the number boards. And though no one actually squealed or had themselves orgies (so far as one could notice in the press) even Brian Epstein could not have arranged more enthusiasm for the Beatles, and the Mayor of Dublin had sent 1,000 shamrocks for distribution by lively Aer Lingus air hostesses.

Tom Dreaper, pink in the face and calm in manner, came slowly down and into the paddock, as the grey clouds let fall some heavy spots of rain. Girls pulled scarves over heads in a rustle of colour. The Duchess' race-glasses swung at the length of their straps, nervously swinging tock-tock, tick-tock. As usual before a Gold Cup the minutes creaked slowly to the start. There seemed ages to wait and nothing to do in them but worry.

The five jockeys burrowed like a group of bright moles through crowds packed twenty deep above the paddock, burst out blinking at the bottom and made their way with little strides and swinging whips – no pockets in breeches to put aimless hands in – towards their owner-trainer complexes.

As Paddy Woods slid the sheet off Arkle's quarters the horse was seen to be sweating slightly but in magnificent condition and absolutely fit. Pat Taaffe was quietly and quickly up on his back and ready to depart but the home-trained Sartorius (Terry Biddlecombe, no less) who had opened at 200 to 1 began to lash out as owner Lt.-Commander Richard Antony Lockhart-Smith, R.N. (Rtd.) seemed to be doing ticklish things to him. The animal's feet flew close by Arkle and Pat Taaffe prudently paused and drew Arkle back. He had won so far £64,422 7s. 6d. from his twenty-three victories in twenty-nine starts. It would have been a pity if Sartorius, hopeful perhaps of even more than the £2,000 second prize, had broken his leg, for apart from anything else, an extra £7,674 10s. looked to be within fifteen minutes of being leisurely earned.

The threat subsided. Arkle made one last progress round receiving with obvious delight the rolling waves of affection, admiration and awe flowing out to him from all sides. He glanced about with an interested superiority as if looking, like Royalty, for a face he should remember and might address.

He had earlier been backed at 110 to 8 and 100 to 9 on as money reached the course via 'the blower', but a few backers now risked money on Lord Cadogan's Snaigow (David Nicholson), double course winner and not without hope in a middle-class handicap. Dormant (Michael Scudamore) now appeared to be trained at home by his owner Mrs. D. M. Wells-Kendrew, a wondrously smart-looking lady, and her husband. His price was 20 to 1. 33 to 1 Capt. Paddy Harbord's Hunch (Stan Mellor) was constant but seldom taken up, but Sartorius for some fantastic reason, or perhaps through the confidence of Lt. Commander Lockhart-Smith was briskly backed by the office agents at all prices from 200 to 1 (a sporting bet against a landslide) down to 50 to 1. After one mile, Sartorius ignorant of his responsibilities and forgetful of what it felt like when he used to win, lost all touch and finished last.

Due off at 4.5 the race started four minutes late, and first Snaigow, then Dormant, led Arkle and the tiny field at a moderate pace. At the eighth fence Arkle took over the lead and came down the hill in front. He had been jumping quickly, neatly and without extravagance, taking the fences economically like a good hurdler and tightly held by Taaffe. So he came to the last fence first time round in front, galloping along without much effort in front of Snaigow and Dormant. But at the instant he reached the take-off point, no take-off happened. He galloped absolutely straight ahead and level and struck the fence flat out with his chest. Birch flew in all directions. Dust and twigs exploded in a brown cloud and Arkle burst through the black birch just above the guard rail like a tank going through a wall. (Picture opposite page 145.)

The shock visibly stopped him. Down plunged his head, up flew his tail in a fountain. Forward shot Pat Taaffe's feet so that his legs to brace himself were almost horizontal and he loosed his left rein and shot his right forward up Arkle's neck to allow him full scope to recover. All this was done in a few film frames.

The intake of 20,000 breaths in a second made a roar like twenty jets and must have upset the peaceful burghers of Gloucester. The next outburst was that clattering release from tension – chatter, giggle, gasp and jest – when an accident has been ducked in the nick. For Arkle had passed through the fence like Moses through the Red Sea: the birch parting to grant him passage and away he went blithely galloping on. It was the most astonishing non-fall. It showed first, his outstanding balance, agility and speed of reaction; secondly, how comfortably within himself he was travelling. It is the tired horse, fully extended, who always falls for a trivial blunder – and Arkle's was a gigantic bog.

As he was coming into the fence his head was high and I thought he was looking straight ahead and high up towards the winning post and the murmuring crowds on both sides of the track. I do not believe he gave a glance downwards at the fence approaching him. His mind was concentrated elsewhere.

Pat Taaffe agrees that Arkle was distracted by people, but he thinks it was by the group crowding in on the left of the fence and just beyond it. Although it felt frightful, Pat never thought he would fall.

Trepidation vibrated as he approached the next fence, the rather staring Open Ditch. But he took off at it, exactly right and swung over with perfect poise and thrust and made his way up hill and round the top and down again followed respectfully by Snaigow as a hunter is followed by his dog. Three fences out he accelerated somewhat and, now utterly on his own in the vast landscape, leapt nimbly over the last fence as if it had never been a nuisance and won in an arrogant canter. Way behind three fences out poor Hunch fell and was killed. Two fences out Snaigow blundered, lost his place, and staggered in so exhausted that David Nicholson had to dismount past the post and wait moments to allow him to recover.

It was left to Dormant to be again second to him, enthusiastically welcomed by the Wells-Kendrews. As hoped for, Arkle had won in a canter by thirty lengths, the longest distance, and at the shortest price in the Gold Cup's history. His time was not particularly good, but it had taken him only 6 minutes 54.2 seconds to earn his money, an income rate of roughly £1,100 a minute (or over £1,500,000 a day).

Johnny Lumley looked utterly exhausted from watching as he padded after Arkle, led by the Duchess, into the unsaddling enclosure. 'But for the shamrock,' he was heard to mutter, 'he was gone for sure.' More shamrock in great tufts was now thrust over the crowd's heads towards Betty Dreaper and the Duchess and Irish voices started to shriek again "dad – hadn't himself rubbed the English noses in the mud again?'

The old, infirm, one-legged and drunk were now hobbling and hopping up the hill to fill the back rows round the sunk unsaddling bowl, elbowing each other viciously for a peep at the marvel under strangers' armpits. They could see that he was barely warm now and had long finished any blowing that was necessary.

Hubbub continued about the unbelievable non-fall.

'I nearly died!' exclaimed the Duchess, and Betty Dreaper, slapping Arkle's neck again and again repeated 'Oh you silly old thing! You silly, *silly* old thing . . . '

A brogue shouted from the crowd: 'Sure, hadn't Saint Patrick had him well backed?' and there was a burst of laughter. 'Audax' of *Horse & Hound*, making a close study of the phenomenon later, discovered almost divine intervention: the birch in the fence was very loose on Wednesday, a 'National Hunt official' ordered it's repair before Thursday. 'But,' 'Audax' informs us 'for one reason or another this, if done at all, was done to only a very small extent. The gratitude of the whole (well nearly the whole) steeple-chasing world is due to the man responsible for, had he obeyed his orders too zealously, no one can say for sure that history might not have been tragically altered.'

Fortunately, such fears for the future of the world did not disturb our hero or his travelling circus. He pulled his way about the unsaddling enclosure in a very cheeky fashion and, long after he'd been led away to the stables to be goggled at again by the lads and girls who look after ordinary horses with equal care, Betty and Tom Dreaper were still signing autographs. The wise old trainer of Kilsallaghan ended top of the list at Cheltenham, and took back £12,612 10s. prize winnings and Arkle's earnings now broke through £70,000. It was noted that the ancient blinkered Sartorius who'd loped around behind had earned, for fourth prize, no less than £516 for Lt.-Commander and Mrs. Lockhart-Smith who thus proved their point in running him.

From racing's brushwood fringe now erupted further cracklings about Arkle's murdering ways: 'Look at poor Hunch –

died there at Cheltenham killed by Arkle's speed!' (But miles behind) 'And what about Snaigow – exhausted to the point of collapse – staggering to a standstill?' (But miles behind).

In any contest it is the placed horses who take the caning.

What one could not do was blame Arkle, any more than one could blame the steep stairs which give an old man heart failure trying to run up them. There are some tasks too large for horses too. Arkle at that moment at level weights was one.

So Arkle returned to Ireland his Gold Cup hat-trick completed with unequalled ease. Two more to emulate Golden Miller . . . But by then he would be eleven. And Flyingbolt was now only seven. Here perhaps, within yards of himself at Greenogue lay a threat greater than middle age. For it was Flyingbolt after his two races at Cheltenham that Tom Dreaper sent to Fairyhouse to try to win his seventh Irish Grand National in succession and his tenth in all. In heavy ground and ridden by Pat Taaffe Flyingbolt, 12 st. 7 lb., beat Height O'Fashion 9 st. 9 lb. (T. F. Lacey this time again) by two lengths. Strictly interpreted, this running makes Flyingbolt 42 lb. superior to Height O'Fashion, exactly the same superiority, except for one neck (worth possibly ⅓rd of a lb.), shown by the unfit Arkle over the mare at Leopardstown on 1st March. On these runnings therefore there are only ounces between the two giants.

Mr. Meredith, handicapper for Sandown's Whitbread Gold Cup for which Arkle had been entered, had produced his weights before the running of the Irish National, giving Arkle 12 stone and Flyingbolt 11 st. 10 lb. There then followed a gap of no less than 30 lb. down to the next horse, What a Myth, the subsequent winner with 9 st 8 lb. only 1 lb. above the minimum, for a horse who had been a heavily-backed second favourite to win the Grand National under 11 st. 4 lb. And after that every horse entered in the race was given under 9 stone. Such is the measure of Arkle's domination.

Torrential rain which caused the abandonment of nearby Epsom for the first time since the 1926 General Strike tumbled on Sandown too. Friday's racing was cancelled, Saturday's was in doubt and Arkle in the circumstances remained at home at Greenogue. Even had he flown over on what then seemed a slim chance of racing, the Dreapers were not too keen on his humping 12 stone around 3 miles 5 furlongs in heavy ground. He was withdrawn on Friday and his presence was much missed by the public, racecourse executive and press – by everyone except the connections of What a Myth and the placed horses Dormant (13 lb. overweight at 10 st. 6 lb.), Kapeno and Kilburn who were thus able to collect considerable wads of Whitbread money.

One of Dreaper's five winners at his favourite Fairyhouse was Arkle's nephew Vulture, the four-year-old son of Cherry Bud, Bright Cherry's daughter whom the Bakers had so wisely kept back at Malahow. This was the first representative of Bright Cherry's grandchildren to run, and he won first time out, a much brighter start than that of his uncle. For the young nephew too the first race was a 'Bumper' for amateurs on the Flat, the 2¼ mile Ballyhack Plate, the customary Dreaper introduction. 'He'd never had his head in front before,' reported Betty Dreaper, 'So he ran as green as grass. We were very thrilled. The way he came up through a large field of horses, was headed in the straight, but fought back again, was very pleasing.' Not greatly fancied at 9 to 1 (he was known to be backward and inexperienced) he finally won by 1 lengths. There was no doubt at all that the youngster had inherited at least a few of his uncle's talents and had valued himself on his first run in excess of the stiff price of 4,600 guineas paid for him by General Mellon to the Bakers. The 'Bumper' itself was an exceptionally valuable one of £449 5s. and, carrying his penalty, he ran well to be third in the Cooltrim Plate worth £511 10s. at Punchestown. When a young horse first wins early in his career, his value leaps far beyond the stakes gained. If he is handsome and does it well and courageously he can double in price. If he is related to the Champion, he is beyond value.

Arkle now at the peak of his career retired as usual for his summer's rest. He had now won one flat race, four hurdle races and 21 steeplechases to the total value of £72,383.

Fourteen

Since 1960 when Anne, Duchess of Westminster had sent her new three-year-old Arkle across the sea to her Cheshire home to be broken in by Lord Wigg's brother-in-law, Bill Veal, the horse had spent all his summers on her 700 acre farm near Maynooth in County Kildare.

The place, like most Irish country properties, is visually difficult, but audibly easy to find. There are few signposts down Irish lanes on the reasonable assumption that if you are on a back way you must either be a local (and know your position without ugly signs) or that, if you are a stranger and patient, some countryman will come along and tell you.

So Bryanstown lies in complete obscurity well south of the main road from Dublin to Mullingar and the West. Suitably enough it lies handily between the Dreapers' stables to the north-east and Pat Taaffe's home to the south.

The front gate is well-kept but not imposing. The drive, which continues the direction of its approaching lane, swings right to disclose suddenly (as drives to country houses should) a pleasant house set among trees, level lawns and brilliant flower-beds. The Duchess moves frequently between Eaton Lodge in Cheshire and Bryanstown throughout the summer. 'I come back and forth a great deal.' She was thus able to keep a literally close eye on her beloved horse: his paddock, now known as 'Arkle's Field', was then called 'The Garden Paddock' for it immediately adjoins the bottom of her garden.

The man who had the care of Arkle every summer from 1964 and for the too-short years of his retirement, was Johnny Kelly.

Kelly, the Duchess' stud groom at Bryanstown, runs the horse side there basically single-handed with help when needed from the farm men. His neat cottage, where he lives with his wife Betty and some of his seven children, sits precisely at the end of the long row of boxes, looking down the yard.

Born on 16th January, 1930 near Kilcock in Co. Meath, Kelly came to Bryanstown in January, 1964. 'It was that March Arkle won his first Gold Cup,' he recalls happily, seeing, as superstitious horsemen will, something fortunate about his arrival. 'But I'd seen him run twice before I came here. I saw him at Fairyhouse—the Power Gold Cup in April, 1963—and I liked what I saw that day. I thought he had the makings of a *great* horse.'

The champion had not then become famous outside Ireland. Arkle had won that race, as he won all his last four races that season, at long odds-on. But so far he had raced only twice in England: when he had won his first steeplechase, the Honeybourne, at Cheltenham; and when, at the same place four months later, he won the Broadway Novices Chase.

Arkle's summer routine at Bryanstown was, until his accident, always the same. It was much in keeping with, and even more casual in some cases than that adopted for all jumpers. The Dreapers would 'rough him off', taking about a fortnight to strip all his rugs off, cut down his food, and lead him out.

The Duchess would then send for him from Kilsallaghan in her Rice trailer pulled by her Jaguar.

Meg, the Duchess' well-known grey hunter would be turned out already in the Garden Paddock, waiting for him. Arkle would come straight out of his trailer into the field and be loosed off. He would go sprinting round the great flat field, disturbing the heavy flocks of cawing rooks in the tall trees which lined its sides. Meg would follow in a sensible, matronly fashion and very soon they would settle down together. The first few moments always used to alarm Johnny Kelly a little.

Arkle stayed out day and night for as long as April as lingered, and for all of May. He got no extra feeding of any sort for the first 14 days. 'Mr. Dreaper,' Johnny Kelly explains, 'always said that the first grass was like a good physick. Then after the fortnight, we'd start feeding him oats, vitamins and minerals and stud-cubes when they came in.

'If the flies were wicked in July we'd bring him and the others in by day and turn them out at night.'

Arkle's box, for no particular reason at first, was near the middle of the long line. Later it was going to be specially equipped with infra-red lamps.

Kelly often rode Arkle out for a few days round the roads before he went back into training. 'He was always very quiet and never any trouble.' Then Arkle would set off in the trailer, a slight change from the large horse-boxes and aircraft in which he grandly cruised about during his racing life.

There were discussions in the summer of 1966 about a possible tilt at the French 'Grand National', the *Grand Steeple' de Paris* at Auteuil, the following summer. The Duchess sought the advice of Fred Winter whose bridleless triumph in that race on Mandarin in June, 1962 is a *tour de force* likely to remain a racing legend all this century.

With the 1967 plan in mind the Duchess paid a visit to Auteuil in the summer of 1966 to watch the racing and check on the course. She saw no reason herself why her wonder horse would not be able to act over and through those eccentric French obstacles. Pat Taaffe, who nurtured a burning ambition to win the Aintree Grand National on Arkle, declared, 'I see no reason why he shouldn't adapt himself. He is very *clever*.'

Peter O'Sullevan commented, 'He's so intelligent, that it might only be necessary to run through a film recording of Mandarin's *Grand Steeple* for his elucidation!'

Tom Dreaper did not, however, enthuse. In the two previous years Arkle, after preliminary first-time-out victories (at Gowran Park and in Sandown's Gallaher Gold Cup respectively) had won Newbury's Hennessy Gold Cup. This, thought Tom Dreaper, should be his first main target again in 1966 and in 1967, too. To be running the horse in France in June when he ought to be resting in his field in Ireland would, Dreaper advised, be a serious disadvantage for his next winter's campaign. The Duchess agreed. The great horse was only nine. There lay ahead the likelihood of at least one more Cheltenham Gold Cup, probably two more, and possibly even three. Mandarin, Cottage Rake and Tom Dreaper's Prince Regent had already all won the race at the age of 11. Silver Fame had been 12.

And Arkle was, *par excellence*, a great 'rester'. He would lie for hours flat out in the Bryanstown sunshine, allowing the Duchess to sit by his dozing head to feed him lumps of sugar as he basked. For successful horses, as for successful human beings, the ability to relax, unwind and rest, is vital. He went back, 'big as a brood mare', as Pat Taaffe reported, to prepare himself for a triple Hennessy victory in November. Pat used to slip across frequently to have a look and a chat. It was not surprising that Arkle was fat. Having missed the Whitbread at Sandown in April due to the heavy ground, he had not raced since his third successive Gold Cup on March 17th. This meant he would have been nearly three-quarters of a year off the course when he appeared at Newbury.

To make matters worse he suffered a minor injury in training at exactly the wrong time. 'He gave himself a cut schooling,' said old Tom Dreaper to me in the spring of 1975, a few days before that grand old man died. 'He missed a weeks work.' Betty Dreaper added, 'And it was at that vital time—14 days before the race.'

If more of the English trainers had known of Arkle's set-back they might have launched their horses against him.

The handicap for the Hennessy presented its extraordinary but regular appearance whenever Arkle figured: 'himself' at the very top, this time with 12st 7lbs, and almost all the rest at the very bottom, this time with 10st. Only one horse in the handicap, What a Myth, was left to carry more than the minimum. A winner already that season (and a future Cheltenham Gold Cup winner, what would be more) he had been burdened with the huge weight of 10st 2lbs.

His trainer, sagacious Ryan Price, did not however consider

that receiving even 30 lbs from Arkle was enough. 'I will not run What a Myth' he declared, 'if Arkle runs. It's up to them to decide. They have the great public horse and it's their responsibility.'

Tom Dreaper's and the Duchess' slight doubts about Arkle's set-back were dissipated. Though distinctly on the heavy side, he was back in work. He would run. As soon as the decision was announced the opposition disintegrated. Whereas in pre-Arkle days fields of 20 and more had contested the Hennessy Gold Cup, only five would now turn out to take him on at Newbury. And this, although he had not run for over eight months, was known to have been held up in his work, and had been beaten in this race on this course by Mill House in 1963.

Lady Weir's What a Myth was in the field after all, fit from an early victory over Rutherfords in a three mile condition chase at Huntingdon a month earlier, and slightly fancied at seven to two against the odds-on Arkle.

The popular northern horse Freddie had some supporters at 13 to 2. The winner in earlier seasons of 10 staying steeplechases, he had already been out three times that autumn before the Hennessy and won twice more, including the £4,971 Gallaher Gold Cup at Sandown, a victory which had earned him a 7 lb penalty now, making his weight 10 st 7 lbs.

Kellsboro' Wood, second to Freddie in the Gallaher, and Master Mascus who had finished last in that race were two more of the runners.

The fifth of Arkle's opponents was the seven-year-old grey gelding Stalbridge Colonist who had passed an interesting summer. Under 9 stone 11 lbs he had been second in the £7,959 Prix des Drags at Auteuil in June, fallen at Enghien in September and then, only a week before the Hennessy, had run tailed off last at Ascot behind Arkle's stable-mate Dicky May.

But from 15 starts in the previous season Stalbridge Colonist had won no less than 11 races: two hurdle races and nine 'chases up to two and a half miles. That battery of victories, however, did not prevent him being given 10 stone minimum in the Hennessy. To win 11 races in 12 months and still be considered the maximum range of the handicap below Arkle ...

The brilliant grey indeed would, only four months later, nearly win the Cheltenham Gold Cup. He was to be beaten only $\frac{3}{4}$ of a length by Woodland Venture.

That November day at Newbury he had on his back an explosive charge in the small but immensely powerful frame of Stan Mellor, almost certainly the greatest lightweight steeplechase jockey ever, and a man who could sometimes conjure out of an exhausted horse an astonishing race-winning leap at the last.

The strength of Stan Mellor, three times Champion jockey with 1,034 winners in his 20 years riding career, would turn out to be the dynamic turning-point of Arkle's undoing at Newbury.

In the paddock Arkle was, as usual, the cynosure of a goggling crowd. He was himself as happy as ever to be back among his public. The attendance on that damp November day was immense. The going, though officially described as 'yielding' on both days, rode fast. On the first day all the races were won in quicker than average times, and the winners included two future champions in Woodland Venture and Persian War. Newbury, one of the fairest of British courses in both senses of the word, always attracts good horses.

Tom Dreaper did not come over. He went racing close home at Navan, saddling two winners: White Abbess for Lord Bicester, and Fort Leney (yet another future Gold Cup winner) for Colonel (now Sir John) Thomson.

Arkle at Newbury was very fresh. In spite of his 12 st 7 lbs and with just over three and a quarter miles to cover he determined to make all the running. Pat Taaffe decided not to fight him, but to accept it. Freddie and Kellsboro' Wood followed him along, with What a Myth making three bad mistakes. The race, as usually happens at Newbury, came to its crunch approaching the first fence in the final straight, in this case the 18th, four fences from home.

At this point What a Myth came under hard driving from

Paul Kelleway. Kellsboro' Wood (Johnny Haine) seemed the most obvious danger to Arkle, but just behind them the grey Stalbridge Colonist (who had been waited with to conserve his known two mile speed) was rapidly making up ground.

So they came down the last four fences, a plain fence, the open ditch, then two more plain ones into the mounting roar of the crowd which at Newbury on a good day extends for more than a quarter of a mile.

Arkle was still just leading going to the last, but Stalbridge Colonist with 35 lbs less on his back was closing on him very quickly.

Pat Taaffe glanced across at Stan Mellor and saw that Stan, sitting down and riding like a dervish, was going for one of those famous last-fence catapults of his. Nearly nine years later Pat recaptured the instant. 'If Stan had been just a *bit* easy on his horse going to the last, he'd not have beaten me. But you know how Stan was! *Everything* going as he went to the last!'

That momentum shot the grey ahead. But Arkle, lacking peak fitness, burdened with weight, having done all the donkey-work (to use an impertinent phrase) was not yet surrendering. He came again heroically up the long run-in with its slight right-handed swerve to miss the water, seemed to the crowd's anguished screams to be nearly there, and went under at the post by a mere half a length. The normally dispassionate comments of *Chaseform* ended 'v. game.'

It was a triumphant failure. But Arkle's public were not only proud, but angry. Protests erupted verbally and in the press at the injustice of the weights now piled upon their hero's back. The sight of him struggling valiantly but vainly up Newbury's run-in, lingered on in the minds of the millions who had been bawling for him on the course and in front of television sets.

The winner, then owned by Mr. R. J. R. Blindell, and trained at nearby Compton by ruby-faced Ken Cundell was the outsider of the field at 25 to 1. He paid nearly 50 to 1 on the Tote and the forecast paid just over £18. Mr. Blindell was enriched by £5,713 10s. Arkle flew back to Ireland.

Fifteen

ARKLE WAS back in England two and a half weeks later for the three mile S.G.B. 'Chase at Ascot on 14th December. The race, worth £2,823, was again a handicap, and Arkle as usual carried 12 st 7 lbs. He had not now carried less than 12 stone for three years. It had been his minimum weight in his last 17 races. Of these he had won every one, except his last Hennessy and the 1964 Massey-Fergusson when he had been asked to carry 12 st 10 lbs over two miles five furlongs only seven days after winning the three and a quarter mile Hennessy.

December had been particularly wet. In very heavy going at Cheltenham on the 10th December, Stalbridge Colonist had carried 11 st 6 lbs in the Massey-Fergusson and finished third to The Laird and Charlie Worcester. Dicky May, favourite though carrying top-weight of 12 st 3 lbs (Mill House was making his reappearance under 12 st) had run disappointingly.

Windsor on the same day had been waterlogged off. Ascot was in doubt. The ground was very heavy and Arkle had only four opponents, the majority carrying the customary 10 stone minimum. Only Master Mascus carried more, with 10 st 3 lbs. Stan Mellor this time rode the useful Vultrix who was second favourite at 9 to 2 to Arkle's 3 to 1 *on*. Vultrix had won this very race in 1965, carrying no less than 2 st 1 lb more, another measure of Arkle's extraordinary supremacy.

The horse for the first time appeared unplaited in the paddock. His mane flew free as he again surveyed his fans with the air of a friendly king. Betty Dreaper explained, 'Plaiting his mane now makes him sweat up a little. And that wastes his nervous energy.'

Arkle again set off to lead all the way. There was, from the way he soared over the fence in front of the stands a rocket-tank of nervous energy to spare. Someone shouted: 'Like a spring-board!' He continued to lead and strode home to win by a very easy 15 lengths. Stan Mellor pursued Arkle over the first 17 fences where Sunny Bright took over Vultrix's depressing task. 'What a horse Arkle must be!' Mellor commented afterwards. 'When I thought I could close up on him I was going as fast as I could, and he just shot away, as if he's only been cantering before. He's a *tremendous* horse.'

Ryan Price was in the unsaddling enclosure as Pat Taaffe rode Arkle in. 'That horse is a living phenomenon!' he exploded. Vultrix who had last year won under 12 st 1 lb, now plodded home third, beaten a casual 18 lengths by Arkle who gave him 35 lbs.

Arkle's victory thrust his winnings past the £75,000 mark, a record which would remain, during a period of steadily rising prize-money, until Comedy of Errors' Champion Hurdle win more than eight years later.

But there was an anxious stooping of backs round Arkle as Pat started to slip his saddle off. There was a cut on his near-fore, the result of another over-reach from one of his over-exuberant leaps. It had fortunately missed the tendon.

Ken Cundell came up and said generously, 'If you'd managed to get another week's work into him before the Hennessy, Stalbridge Colonist would *never* have beaten him.'

Arkle had been in Betty Dreaper's quiet words, 'very impressive.' Although there were only 12 days till he was due to defend his King George VI 'Chase title at Kempton, he again flew back to Ireland. He was now offered at the incredible price of 7 to 1 *on* his winning again on Boxing Day. Looking back on that Ascot race after eight and a half years Pat Taaffe had some strange doubts. 'I just think that something may have happened—or it may have *started* to happen—to him at Ascot.' He looked at me significantly: 'He jumped to the *left* down all those last three fences at Ascot,' he said. He meant that Arkle was jumping away from his off-fore, away from the pedal-bone which was going to crack at Kempton.

'He could have given that foot a tap at Ascot,' said Pat. 'I said something after the race about his jumping.' Jumping left could have caused the over-reach. Perhaps a slight crack did start at Ascot. Nothing, of course, outwardly showed.

Tom Dreaper decided to go to Leopardstown on December 26th where the Duchess was running Corrie-Vacoul against his stable companion Fort Leney in the big Christmas 'Chase. So Betty Dreaper set off with her 15-year-old son Jim* and Pat Taaffe. As there were few 'planes over the holiday period they had to cross on Christmas Eve, and they stayed in the faded grandeur of the Irish Club in Eaton Square. 'It was the first time I'd seen London properly,' said Betty Dreaper, laughing. 'Because it was empty.'

It was also cold. On Christmas night, the Sunday, it froze and racing at Kempton on Boxing Day was postponed for a day. The Irish party took the disruption of their plans philosophically. Jim and Pat Taaffe went off to watch a football match and Betty took herself to the Festival Hall to hear the Nutcracker Suite—'which I enjoyed enormously.'

Arkle and Johnny Lumley remained patiently at Kempton Park. They would, they thought, be a day later getting back to Kilsallaghan. No one could suppose that Arkle's box at Kempton was going to prove his hospital bed for two anxious months.

News just before Christmas that Arkle's old rival Mill House might run against him once again—the big horse had been suffering muscular trouble—caused Arkle's ante-post price to ease from 7 to 1 on to 5 to 1 on, as Mill House was offered at 8's. In the event Mill House waited another month before running a cracking third under 12 st 3 lbs in Doncaster's Great Yorkshire 'Chase.

Arkle was opposed on a grey misty day at Kempton by only

* Now, of course, an immensely successful trainer himself, whose horses won £36,590 in Britain in the 1974/75 jumping season.

six contestants of which only Woodland Venture (backed from 7 to 1 to 6's) was considered to pose the slightest threat.

I ran in the race the charming chestnut horse Maigret who won for us a number of decent long distance 'chases round Sandown and Kempton. I had bought him in Ireland for my friend and writing colleague in the cinema and theatre worlds, Frank Launder, who then shared him with his partner Sidney Gilliatt. Maigret had a very bad heart and was twice resuscitated by the equine heart-expert Mrs. Sally Ann Glendinning. He had therefore to be run very seldom, yet one hundred per cent fit and also one hundred and five per cent fresh. He was thus easily the most difficult horse I ever had the fun of training.

He liked to bowl along in front. Putting to Frank my plan to run against the almighty Arkle in the King George VI I explained: 'We couldn't beat Arkle if we started five minutes earlier. But he will probably scare most of the rest away, giving us a chance of third or fourth money. In the race he'll probably screech off in front. If we tell Johnny Haine to let them go, Maigret will think he's leading the rest and winning!'

The plan tickled Frank's sense of humour and, so far as we were concerned, worked out pretty well as expected. My eyes were naturally split between the illuded Maigret proudly leading the back contingent several fences in the rear, and the drama besetting Arkle at the front.

A few thousand normally attend a Kempton winter meeting. Boxing Day is the track's biggest day of the jumping season, and this time they again had the greatest draw possible: the star of the racing world. There was a gigantic crowd of 16,000 at Kempton, some of which had made the early journey through the traffic jams, because the course was flirting with a very restricted Pay T.V. experiment. Only a few homes in some London boroughs were connected to the system. The rest of Britain and Ireland had to wait for the result or, if they wished to glimpse their hero, turn up at Kempton to watch. The course, never exactly a bower of roses, was then less hideous. It had yet to be scarred by the lucrative gravel workings which later occupied its centre.

In order to gaze at Arkle many racegoers in the members stand neglected the preliminary £2,000 National Hunt Centenary Cup Hurdle won by Terry Biddlecombe on Saucy Kit. Arkle was found beyond the paddock walking in that one pleasant piece of meadowland lined with tall trees and containing the semblance of a ghostly Edwardian cricket pavilion.

Even the conditions of the King George VI, one of 'chasings semi-classics, still gave Arkle his usual 12 st 7 lbs to carry. But nothing else could carry less than 11 stone. These, of the seven runners, included Foinavon (who was going to be the astounding 100 to 1 winner of the Grand National three months later) and Dormant, a chestnut gelding then rising ten who had shown promise and ability three years earlier, had endured sudden moves among several trainers and now appeared at Kempton trained by his owners Mr. and Mrs. Wells-Kendrew of Dorking, Surrey. He had been beaten a distance by Arkle in this race in 1965.

As Arkle walked out onto the course below the winning-post to the left of the stands, the crowd gave him an ovation.

Arkle again set out to lead which, round Kempton's easy circuit and giving for once only 21 lbs. away, was the proper tactic. But Pat Taaffe almost immediately felt something wrong. 'At the second fence,' he recalled, 'which was then the open ditch, Arkle jumped to the left. And that was very strange. . .'

In Pat's mind, of course, niggled the memory of Arkle jumping left down the last three fences at Ascot, the 'wrong' way on both right-handed courses.

'But after that', Pat remembered, 'he seemed O.K. . . . at least till the seventh from home . . . but he was never jumping brilliantly, you know.'

So we all observed with some anxiety. Kempton's fences were then exceptionally stiff. Dunkirk had been killed here in this race a year earlier. And if Arkle repeated at Kempton the nonsense he had made of that softened fence in the Cheltenham Gold Cup . . .

He led for the first circuit and past the post. On the sharp right-handed bend away towards the water he caused a *frisson* of surprise to whistle through the crowds. He momentarily slowed-up. Jeff King on Dormant overtook him and led him away from us over the water-jump to start the second circuit. With hindsight and armed with Pat Taaffe's Ascot recollections it seems possible that the quick right-hand turn may have caused Arkle extra pain.

But by the next fence, which had been the first after the start, Arkle had taken back the lead again. With Woodland Venture now joining Dormant just behind him (and Maigret pleasantly still in touch) he led away from home. There were then three fences on the left side of the course and only two, not three as now, in the straight. He turned right again and then—'At the first along the back', says Pat, 'he went *right through it*. Being Arkle, of course, he could always find a fifth leg, but . . .' Pat hunches those huge stooping shoulders of his.

I hear in my ears still that shocked inrush of ten thousand 'Ooohs . . !'

Woodland Venture, swooping upon Arkle's blunder, went past him and led him over the next open ditch past the stables. But Arkle was rallying, getting back in the race and by the next fence, the second last on the far side, he led again. Dormant had made a mess of the last fence on the left, the one before Arkle's grave mistake and now together with Maigret seemed out of the hunt. If anything could trouble Arkle it could only be Woodland Venture. Arkle's optimistic fans murmured to themselves 'He'll soon leave that one.' But among the experts, the more cynical, the less chauvinistic, nasty doubts began to gnaw. Through our glasses it was horribly plain that Arkle, so far from playing with his rival, was, for some strange reason, not going all that the better.

Arkle and Woodland Venture duelled in front. Then to everyone's surprise and to most of our anguish, Terry Biddle-combe pushed Woodland Venture past Arkle yet again and was leading at the seventeenth, the last fence on the far side, before the long run round the final bend towards the two fences then remaining in the straight.

Going to the second last fence Arkle had won the ground back again. But he had not snatched it back like a panther. He had regained it grimly. He was pegging back Woodland Venture not by the brilliant acceleration of a wonder horse but by a dour struggle. No one in the stands knew, nor did Pat on his back know, of the terrible pain increasing and increasing in his off-fore foot, jabbing with darts each time the foot touched the ground, lancing with agony as he landed over the fences.

Arkle had an immense pride. He was accustomed to superiority. His blood was up. Like the valiant soldier accustomed to victory it had never occurred to Arkle to surrender. He battled on now.

'At the second last,' Pat remembers, 'I saw Terry coming at me once again and I was just thinkin' "I can knock him off", when he fell, and I was left alone.'

It did not immediately seem to us in the stands that Arkle then started to weaken. We saw Dormant rounding the bend into the straight still far behind, but plainly and amazingly closing on the favourite. It seemed then, for no one could imagine Arkle slowing down, that Dormant must be accelerating. In retrospect we know that Dormant was simply plugging on at the same pace, but that the pain in Arkle's foot had caused him finally to put less weight upon it, and to shorten his stride.

Arkle was all alone now in that grey December dusk in the depths of the year. The crowd was roaring for him, bellowing at him from those great grey whales of stands with the lights aglimmer in the bars. But there was one more fence to jump, another quarter of a mile of pain . . .

'Going to the last,' says Pat, 'he did start changing his legs. I knew then something was wrong. But he was *not* pulling up. Even then, he was not pulling up.' The years have not diminished by one grain the jockey's loving admiration of his horse.

'We came to the last,' said Pat, 'and he *still* jumped it and made for the line and it was only in the last fifty yards that he started the stop.'

Arkle had jumped the last fence crookedly to the left—anything to take the weight off his off-fore. On landing he had dwelt, hesitated and probably wondered whether he could still keep on. But again he set off. Taaffe, to stop him hanging, had raised his whip in his left hand.

'Then Dormant,' says Pat Taaffe, 'came at him on the stands side and that was that. And of course I left him alone.'

Arkle had pulled himself up to a trot as he passed his final winning-post. He was very lame walking in. As he stood between Dormant and Maigret for Pat to slip the racing-saddle and weight cloth off his back for the last time, he was crippled. Pat Taaffe's face was twisted with his grief. He just whispered, 'His leg's gone. He's broken down.'

There was a dreadful silence all round the unsaddling enclosure.

Holding his hot saddle Pat had to squeeze past the desperately enquiring pressmen to weigh-in. 'What happened? What is it? Is it bad, Pat? When, Pat?'

Taaffe had no idea what was so gravely wrong. But he said firmly, 'It happened at that second fence. Where he jumped left. I think he galloped all those three miles in pain.' To further questions he replied, 'He was hanging all the time . . . never really going well. No, his jumping wasn't the same.'

Ryan Price came forward to the desolate group around the stricken Arkle. He said, 'I'll look after him.' That offer glowed in Pat Taaffe's memory ever since. Henry Hyde of Kempton immediately offered the use of the racecourse stables for as long as Arkle might need them. Ryan Price suggested an X-ray. Someone knew of a local firm, Portable X-Rays Limited, from nearby Chiswick. Arrangements were made by the racecourse veterinary surgeons to have X-rays taken at all speed. By 3.45 four plates were taken. By 5 p.m. Arkle's own vet, the late 'Maxie' Cosgrove had been contacted in Ireland. He arranged to fly over next day. In the meantime Arkle's front shoes had been removed by course blacksmith Ron Warner for an immediate external examination. It revealed nothing. The horse ambulance was brought as close as possible to the unsaddling enclosure to save Arkle the long walk across the course to the stables. Arkle could hardly hobble to it, and up into it. The Duchess and Betty Dreaper saw him safely re-installed in his box in the racecourse and then flew from London to Cheshire and Co. Dublin respectively. The Duchess would be back next day at Kempton to confer with Maxie Cosgrove.

December dusk had fallen like a pall. In the encircling gloom the lights from the damp and shadowy stands gleamed like tears. It seemed to some of us then to be the tolling end of an era.

Sixteen

TOM DREAPER however, racing at Leopardstown, had no idea what had happened to his great horse. 'I saw the English results go up on the board,' he said, 'and I saw Arkle was second, but I couldn't understand what had gone wrong. And then, a while later, I think it was Michael O'Hehir' (the famous commentator) 'who came up to me and said "Arkle finished lame".' With this grim uncertainty Dreaper had to live until the evening.

Pat Taaffe, who had left Kempton believing Arkle's tendon had broken down, was at Heathrow hurrying for his 'plane home at 6 p.m. when he heard the news on someone's transistor radio and read it in the evening papers. It stood out boldly on the front pages. The first of many veterinary bulletins was released. The X-rays had been examined. Arkle had cracked his pedal-bone and might never race again.

Betty Dreaper was tackled by the fretting press on her return to Greenogue. She said, 'The X-ray revealed that Arkle has fractured a bone in his off-fore hoof. There is a 50—50 chance of recovery. But he certainly won't race again this season.'

Over the next weeks shoals of X-ray photographs would be taken in Arkle's box in the empty racecourse stables at Kempton. Four veterinary surgeons would come to consult over his case, including his own practitioner, the late and eminent Maxie Cosgrove from Dublin and the renowned Mr. James Roberts then of Newmarket's Equine Research Station. Cosgrove was there by 3 p.m. on Wednesday, flying in to Heathrow from Dublin as the Duchess flew back from Cheshire. Cosgrove studied the X-ray plates. He was grim. 'The break is a bad one,' he said. He set to work preparing to fix a 5 lb. plaster cast round Arkle's leg from the knee down to protect Arkle's foot from the real danger of further knocks. The task took him $1\frac{1}{2}$ hours.

Back in Ireland Cosgrove's partner, James Kavanagh, who was going to be in charge of all the X-rays on Arkle over the next two and a half years was already examining the first plates.

'I didn't need to be "called in",' Kavanagh corrected me eight and a half years later in his modern house at Castleknock just beyond Dublin's lovely Phoenix Park. 'Arkle's accident was public knowledge on the radio and television the night it happened. Ah, *everybody* knew about it.'

Together we pore over the photographs of Arkle's broken foot.

James Kavanagh explains, pointing to the crack, 'One third of the pedal-bone—the "outside" third of the off-fore—was broken away. That crack is between two and a quarter inches and two and a half inches long. Now pedal-bones are bad ones to crack. For though the bone is encased in the hoof which makes a natural sort of cast around it, stopping the piece *moving*, as you might say, the bone itself receives a poor blood supply. This makes it not a good area for union. You get some degree of union, but not a lot.'

In layman's terms, broken bones join together by the production of something which is the basis of an ultimate boney deposit. It makes first a fibrous union, which should then calcify, becoming a sort of cement. 'You get a fibrous union,' says Kavanagh, 'but not often the solid boney sort of union you get in *long* bones.'

In Arkle's case later X-ray photographs showed that the union became partly calcified, but not sufficiently so to ensure a complete, permanent union. There were thus soon the bulletins suggesting the possibilities of an operation. This would then have entailed opening up the hoof, screwing the fractured pedal-bone together with vitallium metal screws, sealing over the hole in the hoof again with a plastic material and then waiting months for the hoof to grow over it again. An operation would be difficult and lengthy. If the bone would knit together on its own, it would be an easier proposition. The constant danger remained that any movement or small knock could cause further displacement of the cracked-off third of the pedal-bone. On the day after the accident Maxie Cosgrove declared at Kempton: 'He shouldn't be moved for at least six weeks'.

Kempton's stabling manager, Jim Hogg, made Arkle most welcome. The Duchess said goodbye to Arkle and went sadly home. Cosgrove went back to Ireland. That night Jim Hogg gave the news about his guest. 'He's settled down well,' he said, 'He doesn't appear to be in much pain.'

The only way Arkle's veterinary surgeons could relate any progress was by taking a series of X-ray plates. A comparison of these would show if a union was beginning. After a while they did.

The progress of the invalid was followed with as much attention as that given to an ailing Prime Minister or an injured pop star.

Arkle's fame and public anxiety promoted news of him beyond the confines of the sports pages. *The Times* carried his veterinary bulletins on its front page. Feature writers, not always completely *au fait* with equine terminology, outstrove each other in rival popular dailies to bring their readers a frequent record of Arkle's struggle to recover. In health he was big news; in sickness even more so. News of the stricken hero was eagerly sought.

No other steeplechaser since Golden Miller had so ensnared the public's hearts. Gifts, get-well cards, telegrams, Christmas cards, cases of stout, toys and packets of sweets, some envelopes and parcels simply addressed to '*The Champion, Kempton*,' made their way from all parts of the world to the otherwise empty racecourse stable block near Sunbury-on-Thames. If the Irish postmen could cope with the simple address "*Arkle, Ireland*," their British counterparts could do just as well. The cards and letters soon overflowed the door of Arkle's box. A plywood hoarding was discovered, placed against his stable wall and was soon fully decorated with more than one hundred greetings cards. The majority came from punters, but several were dispatched by other animals, including children's ponies. One was from a dog called Prince. The Duchess reported proudly, 'He's had far more cards than I had.'

Anne, Duchess of Westminster flew frequently from her Cheshire and Scottish homes to London to call on Arkle. For the major veterinary conferences in the Kempton stable-yard, Betty Dreaper flew over from Ireland. Press and photographers were in constant but quiet attendance. The 'intrusion into private grief' of which reporters are sometimes accused, did not include any disturbance of the equine superstar. They were never any trouble and what they had to say was eagerly awaited. Arkle reciprocated the reporters' interest and conducted himself with an intelligent and grateful decorum. This would prove vital to his recovery. Had he proved fractious, let alone panicky, his foot could have been irreparably damaged. As a further protection against the knocks in the box to which all horses' hooves are subject, Cosgrove had encased Arkle's foot and leg from the knee down in the five pound plaster cast. On this stiff stump Arkle moved cautiously about like a man with a newly broken leg. He took care. He minded how he went, and he soon learned how to lie down and get up with it.

One major veterinary press conference took place at Kempton on 7th January, 1967, and was reported on the front page of that day's *Evening Standard*. Further X-rays had been taken and these would show whether, with time and Arkle's weight upon it, the split had lengthened or broadened. If so, the prognosis would be very gloomy indeed. But 'Maxie' Cosgrove was happy to announce:

'We must say this; there has been no deterioration whatsoever, and this is a very pleasing factor.

'There has been no separation in the fractured bone and from the extensive X-raying we have done this morning we are quite happy that the continuity of the bone is intact.

196

'We are no further in helping you as to whether Arkle will race again. This question will not be answerable for another two or three months. The temperament of the animal is ideal. He is not a nervous horse and is allowing the fracture to heal.

'On the whole, our report today is good news. We might have had a separation of the fractured bone and that would have been extremely serious.'

James Roberts of the Equine Research Station, pointed out that Arkle had learned how to get up and lie down without injury to the hoof, so that the whole of the circumstances of the case could not be better.

Both Cosgrove and Roberts agreed that the danger period for Arkle was swiftly approaching. Roberts said: 'In about two weeks' time the fracture will be at its most dangerous state. It is then that it could widen and might separate.'

One of the difficulties of caring for a crippled horse is the maintenance of the right diet. Because the incarcerated animal can take no exercise his food must be cut to a minimum. Surplus energy will otherwise cause him to spring about his box and extend his injuries. Simultaneously, his strength must, like any patient's, be kept up to aid nature's healing process. In Arkle's case it was particularly important to keep the blood supply flowing healthily to the hoof. Bone-meal with added vitamins to boost the calcifying process was added to his diet, which still included his customary swig of Guinness.

As Cosgrove and Roberts had said, Arkle's intelligence saw him out. He was wary. But he fed well. He remained in superb condition. His coat stayed glossy under his dark-blue blanket. His eyes glowed. The credit for his continued health rested entirely with the succession of stable lads from Greenogue who, by arrangement with the Duchess and Tom Dreaper, came over on a rota every week or ten days, so that none might become too bored or lonely in the empty block of the racecourse stables. By the time of the next major conference future jocky Sean Barker had relieved Johnny Lumley and was in charge at Kempton.

'Maxie' Cosgrove warned: 'It is a very serious injury. The fracture is vertical, a very rare break which occurs only about twice a year to racehorses in Britain.

'In six weeks' time we hope it has healed enough to move him back to Ireland, but a lot depends on Arkle himself. If he becomes restless it would take longer.'

He added: 'If the hoof becomes inflamed or there is any other complication it may be necessary to operate. But we will not know for a fortnight.'

The Duchess said, 'We have to wait and see what happens, but up to now Arkle's been the perfect patient. He's been very good about it all. He's physically very, *very* well. There's no deterioration, and that's the main thing.'

Now that Arkle was out of pain, the public kept enquiring when the greatest 'chaser of all time might run again. When might he be seen again in action?

Under some pressure, the Duchess went so far as to repeat Maxie Cosgrove's prognosis and to hope there might now be a '50—50 chance of his racing again.' This phrase was snatched up and lobbed out for a run in the headlines.

Of all Arkle's connections Maxie Cosgrove, his vet, was then and throughout the ensuing years the most optimistic about his chances. Pat Taaffe, his jocky, was and remained the most pessimistic. Through his own body Taaffe had felt Arkle's pain. He had also the suspicion that the injury, having started earlier, perhaps at Ascot, would be much graver and last possibly for ever, as if a split in a post had been gradually widened and deepened by continued hammering.

Back at home in Ireland, Taaffe said: 'Being faithful to the old fellow *I* hope he never races again. As far as I'm concerned talk of a 50–50 chance next year—when he'll be eleven—is wildly optimistic! Most horses are past their peak for 'chasing at that age and whatever happens I don't *want* him to try to make a come-back.

'I couldn't bear to see that fellow try and fail. Arkle has a bigger heart than most *people*. I want to think of him spending the rest of his days enjoying his honourable retirement. He's the finest horse there ever was and there will never be another horse like him.'

But if Arkle did run again?

'Then, of course,' said Pat, 'I'll ride him. But I don't want people to remember the fellow as the horse that *tried* to make a come-back. I want them just to remember him as the best.'

The weeks passed. On 1st February, Pat Taaffe, even then a very senior jockey, suffered a smashing fall at Haydock in the National Trial on Arkle's stable companion Thorn Gate. It was not a lucky time. Pat was going to be out of action for the rest of the season.

Arkle's admirers continued to trek out to Kempton Park to wish him well. Lads from Kilsallaghan came to care for him and went home again. The Duchess paid her fond visits. The veterinary surgeons took X-rays, convened and prognosticated, and the press, radio and television recorded the patient's gradual improvement. On February 6th, after further examination by four vets, and by Tom Dreaper who had flown from Ireland, Arkle's five pound plaster cast was removed by Maxie Cosgrove, using long-handled cutters. To the trepidation of all watchers he promptly got down and rolled, delighted to be at last free of the constriction. He had always loved his rolling. He got up, shook himself and walked soundly across the straw.

Cosgrove announced: 'We couldn't be more pleased. This gives us a little further encouragement that Arkle may go into training again. The X-rays show that the break is healing satisfactorily—the chip of bone, which was causing anxiety, has stayed in place.' The leg, too, looked fine. It was now supported by elastic bandages.

Tom Dreaper was delighted also by Arkle's condition. 'He looks *much* better than I expected,' he said, then added cautiously, 'He'll need a long rest. We'll just hope for the best so far as racing's concerned.'

Then on February 23rd (there was racing at Ascot) it was announced that Arkle's medical advisors at last considered that he could travel home. He would fly back to Ireland the following Sunday, February 26th. It was nearly nine weeks since his accident. The announcement everywhere fanned rising hopes that he might run next season.

He flew as usual to Collinstown, but made his way not that short step northwards to Kilsallaghan but west to Bryanstown. He was going home to convalesce.

In his absence, the result of the Cheltenham Gold Cup simply confirmed Arkle's colossal superiority over ordinary horses. Good horses to whom he had always given away two stone and more disputed the finish: Woodland Venture beat Stalbridge Colonist and What a Myth by threequarters of a length and two lengths. Dormant was fourth. Mill House fell at the seventeenth when leading.

Johnny Kelly at Bryanstown had everything prepared for Arkle's return. Like Tom Dreaper, he had not realised at first the seriousness of Arkle's injury. He had listened to the race on the radio and had been bewildered. 'We wondered what had happened. Seeing it was in a non-handicap we thought he'd lead and never be caught.'

There was a barn at Bryanstown in which the calves had been. There was a deep litter of straw and on this were placed quantities of soft peat-moss, so that the depth of the bed became two feet. Straw-bales lined the walls, lest Arkle should bang into the sides of the big half-open barn.

'Then,' Kelly recalls, 'as he'd have room to be inclined to be lonesome, we put a donkey in there to take the lonesomeness off him.'

The C.I.E. box drove round the back of Bryanston house right up to the barn which lies behind it, part of the complex of farm buildings behind the line of stables.

Nellie, the donkey borrowed from the daughter of the Duchess' caretakers, was awaiting Arkle's arrival. 'He was the sort of horse,' says Kelly, 'who'd take up with anything.'

Kelly had not seen him over at Kempton. When Arkle stepped down the ramp of the box his plaster cast was off and he was shod in front. He went straight into the barn and was let loose. 'He bucked and kicked like anything,' Kelly remembers. 'I feared something would happen.'

In the barn he seemed sound. 'Trottin' up and down in there on the soft he was a hundred per cent. You'd think there was nothing wrong with him. But as soon as he put his feet on concrete,' Kelly says, 'he was definitely lame at the walk. Not *every* step, but you'd notice a step or two.'

Arkle was sent liquid encouragement. Students of the Westminster Hospital to whom the Duchess had presented one of his shoes, reciprocated in June with a crate of beer for him. He was also unwittingly connected with criminal proceedings. The Irish Government had that spring introduced their new half-crown which bore, so properly for Ireland, the emblem of a horse. The sharp boys were soon selling these pieces to fans and tourists as 'Medals of Arkle' at ten shillings a time. This three hundred per cent profit earned one gang a gain of £2,000.

Except for the occasional try-out in the yard for his two vets, Maxie Cosgrove and James Kavanagh to observe, Arkle stayed in his barn all summer. Kavanagh continued to take X-rays to check the slow progress of union. There was no treatment.

Kelly relates, 'Mr. Cosgrove said it just needed time to weld, that there was something that would ooze out of the bone to fix it together. He said that if it welded, it would be so strong there that, if it ever split again, it would be in another place!'

The summer drew on. He was ten now, probably at his prime. But from now on he would be at best only on a plateau of perhaps a season or a year's duration from which his abilities could only decline. In August Pat Taaffe had fully recovered from his fall, and the rest had restored his spirits. 'I want to win again on Arkle,' he declared.

Arkle, apart from Nellie, (they used to chase each other around the barn) had much to entertain him. The corn ripened, and harvest came. Kelly recalls, 'When they were drawing in the corn the tractors were *whizzin'* past the barn, but he didn't mind at all. And there was the corn-drier right next door to him roarin' away!'

On 8th August, after more X-rays, Tom Dreaper sounded the first informed note of real optimism. He declared, 'I feel myself that Arkle will run again. But of course a decision cannot be made till he's been back in my stables for some time.'

The testing time came. Kelly had been leading him out shod in heavy shoes. The improvement was plain. He returned to Tom Dreaper's care at Greenogue in October, ten months since he had left his box there to set out for what had seemed a simple victory at Kempton. The word was out now that 'he was almost certain to run again.' To assist his preparation towards his goal of a fourth Gold Cup, Leopardstown racecourse offered a special condition race framed for his benefit at their February meeting of 1968. Pat Taaffe eight years later remarked, 'And they'd kindly proposed a welter-weight flat race, so that I could ride him!'

An official announcement had been made that, if Arkle did run again, it would never be in another handicap. The news brought comfort to the owners and trainers of those good horses who, without Arkle, would have enjoyed sporting chances of being the stars of their time.

Not everything, however, was going well with Arkle's training. 'He was,' the great Tom Dreaper reflected, '*sometimes* lame. When he was going *off* to canter sometimes. He'd canter alright, but ...' Dreaper's voice trailed off. Something was not absolutely right. Perhaps it was muscular? Or a touch of arthritis? Or rheumatism? Tom Dreaper shrugged. No one had been sure.

The year for Arkle drew disappointingly to its close. It had suffered a horrible start, grown better, sent up green shoots of hope. Now at the end of the year optimism was feeling the frost. But in one gallop in December Paddy Woods (subsequently a sizeable and successful trainer in the village) was hard put to hold Arkle. With Christmas came Arkle's customary benefit of presents, including this year three sticks of rock from Blackpool.

His public continued to call upon him. One visitor in February following the well-beaten backways to Greenogue came upon a Boy Scout: the lad's uniform announced that he belonged to the '1st Arkle Troop'.

An outbreak of Foot and Mouth disease threatened restrictions on racehorse travel between Ireland and England. As a hedge against the continuance of quarantine regulations until the Cheltenham National Hunt Festival, Windsor racecourse offered an alternative 'come-back' race for Arkle on 28th February. Leopardstown with equal generosity and show-business acumen then proposed to run a 'Restoration Stakes' at a special fixture to be held on 6th March.

Everybody was doing their damnedest to help Arkle get right. But time was running out now with depressing speed. As New Year's Day darted past Arkle became eleven years old. The possibility of even running in the 1968 Gold Cup receded faster, faster, then vanished. The plan for his come-back was again postponed: it would now be in the Mosney Hurdle, a condition race over two and a half miles, to be run at nearby Fairyhouse on Easter Tuesday, 16th April. The news of this new target broke in March together with pictures of Pat Taaffe riding work on Arkle. 'He seems to know it's me on him. But this is only meant to be a try-out,' Pat explained, 'to see if he pulls up sound.'

Betty Dreaper was bombarded by requests from distant visitors asking her to try to find them hotel rooms somewhere near, so that they could stay to watch Arkle's return.

As a final step towards the Fairyhouse race Arkle was taken to Naas racecourse to be ridden by Pat Taaffe in a full-scale school over hurdles with his stable-mate Splash.

Taaffe relates the outcome. 'When we pulled up Mr. Dreaper was waitin', and he looked up at me with his head on one side—you know the way he had—and he asked, "All right, Pat?"

'I said, "No, Sir!" Mr. Dreaper asked, "When d'you think he'll be right?" And I said, "I think he'll never be right, Sir." '

The ground grew firm beneath the spring winds and sunshine. Too firm. On 10th April it was announced that hard ground had cancelled his return at Fairyhouse and that a decision on his whole racing future would now have to be postponed until the autumn. An entire season had elapsed.

Arkle's stable companion, Fort Leney, with Pat Taaffe riding, had won the Cheltenham Gold Cup by a neck from The Laird with Stalbridge Colonist a length away third. Mill House, whom Fulke Walwyn had wonderfully rehabilitated, started favourite on this his second appearance of the season and, ridden by Willie Robinson, led all the way till he fell at the fifteenth fence.

Mill House's old conqueror went home again from Greenogue, unraced, to Bryanstown. Even if he could run again for the Gold Cup he would have missed a season and a half out of the summit of his life. By the following March he would be twelve.

I asked Tom Dreaper the week before he died how long he thought Arkle would have gone on. He had started his racing career late, as a great 'chaser should. He had never been bustled, Tom nodded. It was true, too, that with perhaps only three exceptions he had never been subjected to a hard race. Nearly all his 35 contests had been easy ones. Tom Dreaper smiled: Arkle had never been strained. 'He was never asked to do more than he was able.' It was Dreaper's golden rule of training. 'He was at his peak,' said Tom. 'He'd have held on. He was relaxed, you see: he took it very easily.'

'He really did enjoy life,' said Betty Dreaper. Tom said, 'He enjoyed *everything*.'

Seventeen

ARKLE SPENT a lovely summer at Bryanstown with old Meg. A
television company was making another documentary about
him. He received 160 letters on his birthday, and greeted
overseas visitors at Greenogue that spring from ten other
countries.

During the summer the Duchess often rode Arkle round her
farm. 'He was a lovely ride,' she says fondly. 'He'd shove
himself into a ditch for me to get on. Or I'd get on off the
muck-cart—everyone used to laugh—or from the bumper of a
car. He really did look after me.'

But on her first ride on him she was away for so long that
Kelly became worried. 'I thought Her Grace couldn't have
gone far because she wouldn't be able to open any gates,' he
says. The Duchess laughs. 'Well, of course, Arkle had never
opened gates at the Dreapers', but I think you could have
taught that horse *anything*! You could teach him to roll over like
a dog!' Opening the gates as if he were another old hunter, she
and Arkle had ridden all round her farm.

We are sitting on a sunny bank at the edge of her garden. At
our feet lies the path running to the right towards the stables
and left towards his grave. The spring sun of 1975 is warm on
our three faces. 'Was it really only then?' the Duchess wonders,
thinking about those happy rides. She plucks grass from the
bank as she talks, and Kelly is very easy and friendly with her.

'Arkle would gallop and take a strong hold,' says the Duchess,
'but I never *ever* felt he'd run away with me. He really liked

human beings you know much better than horses. Because he absolutely trusted everyone. He was an astonishing horse. When he was lying down in the field or in his box in the straw he'd never get up. He'd only lift his head just enough to lay it on my lap. He knew one's voice. He knew my car driving into the Dreapers and he knew my foot in the yard. He'd start banging on the box door with his toe . . .'

The Duchess so loved having Arkle at Bryanstown and so enjoyed the hours hacking him about and petting him in the field—'She did spoil him dreadfully with those sugar lumps,' says Kelly smiling—that the decision which shook the racing world came to her quite gently.

On the 9th October, 1968, the Duchess formally announced the retirement of the greatest steeplechaser ever. 'Arkle is sound and very well,' she said, 'but, although his come-back had been planned for Leopardstown after Christmas that would be only just short of his twelfth birthday. After a great deal of thought and discussions with Mr. Tom Dreaper and Mr. Cosgrove,' she went on, 'we have decided to retire him. Not even Arkle, with his immense courage,' she concluded, 'could be expected to reproduce his old brilliance . . .'

'Not even Arkle . . .' how often in his life and afterwards that phrase has rung out like a trumpet of salutation, the declaration of a different breed.

The senior Irish handicapper officially rated Arkle three stone superior to Fort Leney who had that spring won the Cheltenham Gold Cup. I am convinced that no other horse will be born who can possibly be rated higher than the maximum range of the handicap above the good and fair winner of steeplechasing's classic crown. 'And even that gap,' commented the handicapper, 'would not have brought them together.'

I had in my care the 1957 Gold Cup winner Linwell, who would almost certainly have won again in 1958 and was then second (a shade unluckily) in 1959. This was a very good horse indeed, noted by John Welcome in his admirable history *The Cheltenham Gold Cup* as a much underrated Gold Cup winner. I know that Linwell's attempt to give 16 lbs. to Mandarin, a subsequent Gold Cup winner, in the first running of the Hennessy was our horse's finest hour. Yet here we have Arkle officially assessed at three times better than that. Incredible.

The Duchess' retirement decision was widely welcomed. Betty Dreaper with her usual simple brevity stated, 'We'd much rather see Arkle in happy retirement than coming in third somewhere, a tired, dispirited horse.'

No word was ever uttered by the Dreapers then, or at the time of Arkle's accident, or at any time since about the magnitude of their disappointment that their champion had been deprived of at least two and a half seasons of his racing life. For the Duchess and for the Dreapers the horse came first.

So he did, but without any personal loss of opportunity, for the rest of us. We who had come not only to admire but really to love him, breathed deep sighs of relief that this phenomenon would now never be risked on a racecourse again. As we had anticipated that mournful grey December day at Kempton twenty-two long months earlier, an era in racing history had been concluded. We had been blessed—and were doubly lucky to know it in his lifetime—to have seen the greatest equine genius of the steeplechasing scene. It comforted us all that he had a gently caring last home in the best of hands. We thought happily and confidently that he would live on there for years and years, enjoying a quiet life and his contented recollections.

But as the winter of 1968 drew in, Arkle began to show more mysterious signs of stiffness. In Kelly's words, 'That autumn we thought he might have arthritis in his hip, and the muscle there started to waste. Sir Charles Strong came over from London to give him muscular treatment. After a bit', Kelly adds, 'I could work the machine on Arkle myself.' This was the faradaism treatment for which Charles Strong became so justifiably famous for his cures of numerous famous horses. There is, in my experience, nothing so beneficial in the treatment of muscular strains and wasting. 'Oh, nothing was spared for Arkle,' says Kelly with pride. 'No time or money was spared to get him right.'

'He seemed,' said the Duchess, 'to be stiff in his back, and it was then, I think, that Maxie Cosgrove began to talk about the possibility of brucellosis. But then,' she added mildly, 'Maxie was talking a lot about brucellosis at that time.'

To keep his back and muscles and bones warm infra-red lamps were installed in Arkle's box. When he was turned out in the winter it was always in a New Zealand rug. With the warmth of spring Arkle seemed less stiff. 'Could it be,' wondered Kelly, 'that the arthritis from his broken foot could go all through his body?'

I asked James Kavanagh about this. He says that, although there is a theory among medical practitioners that this may happen in humans, and there has therefore been talk of it occurring in horses, there is still no proof that it does.

Brucellosis in horses certainly spreads, but Arkle showed none of the other symptoms of this strange disease which some horses and humans pick up from cattle. The old 'poll evil' and fistulous withers are manifestations of the disease which in horses often starts at the fetlock joints. Serological tests on the blood are used to diagnose brucellosis.*

According to James Kavanagh, the British Ministry of Agriculture at Weybridge produce a vaccine exclusively for brucellosis in equines. Kavanagh adds, 'So far as I know it was never confirmed that Arkle had brucellosis. Blood tests can prove negative even when the animal has got brucellosis. Frequently you can isolate it in pure culture from an abscess on the poll or withers.'

In addition to the regular faradaism treatments and to infra-red heat, Arkle also had several courses of drugs of the cortisone type administered by Maxie Cosgrove. Pat Taaffe is inclined to think that he had a great many injections. During the summer Arkle became much easier in his movements.

* From: *The Horse's Health from A to Z* (published by David & Charles) by Peter D. Rossdale MA, FRCVS and Susan M. Wreford. 'Levels of antibody can be measured in serum and expressed in titre, i.e. the lowest dilution of serum at which antigen/antibody reaction occurs in test tube, e.g. in brucellosis 1 in 10 titre is negative and 1 in 40 positive.'

The Duchess rode him frequently and they greatly enjoyed their times together. As a precaution against his catching cold he was turned out, even on some summer days, in one of those splendidly light but warm Lavenham rugs. The Duchess keeps several coloured photographs of him dozing in a blue quilted rug in his paddock, like an elderly lightly-coated gentleman soaking up the spring sun's warmth along the old Promenade des Anglais.

The October of 1969 stayed particularly warm and the onset of Arkle's stiffness was kept at bay. So when the then Colonel 'Mike' Ansell asked the Duchess if Arkle could be paraded at Wembley at The Horse of the Year Show, she willingly agreed. He had not been forgotten. As soon as his appearance was announced, advance bookings leapt 35 per cent on the previous year's.

Arkle, on what would be his last visit to England, stayed a full week. He was based at Lord Knutsford's home near Watford from the Sunday before the show until the Sunday it closed, and he drove in to meet his public every day. On the show ground he had a stable next door to Princess Anne's horse and she looked in to greet him and to talk to Kelly about him. His box was beseiged by his admirers all 6 days and every evening. After the Monday he paraded twice daily. 'He was *delighted* with himself,' says Kelly who led him in, sometimes with Pat Taaffe riding, for the Parade of Personalities. 'Just like he was racin', he'd put his head up and have his ears cocked, looking' at the crowds. The applause was so *enormous*, he'd give a jump when I led him in.'

Pat Taaffe remembers, 'He bowed to Her Grace, who loved it. When he was warmed up from the exercise he felt really well. It is unbelievable to think that he was really so bad.'

The Duchess says, 'All the clapping was right down his street! He adored it. There was a costermonger's cart there, piled with apples and pears. And Arkle absolutely stripped it. I wrote to the owner to apologise and he wrote me the most charming letter back, saying he was delighted and honoured that Arkle had eaten all his fruit.'

Arkle showed off excessively. One night, standing in front of the parade with David Broome's show-jumper, he set about the show's hydrangeas and munched them up.

Mike Ansell had asked the owners of all the personalities to select the tune they would like the band to play each time their horse paraded. The Duchess did not ponder long. She picked for Arkle '*There'll Never Be Another You.*'

Arkle had always played to his public. Like a politician before a crowd and an actor in the theatre he needed acclamation. In his case he deserved it. But, just as public performers come off drained of nervous energy having given their all, so Arkle gave great performances all that Wembley week. And it was probably the reaction from that, coupled with the onset of the cold winter that brought on him very soon an increasing degree of stiffness.

This may sound more like the symptoms of arthritis, but it is true, too, that brucellosis in horses comes and goes in waves, flaring up and subsiding like the effects of glandular fever in humans.

Arkle grew stiff. He was not, in the opinion of James Kavanagh who accompanied his partner Maxie Cosgrove on visits to Bryanstown, actually lame. He was 'more "*pottery*", like we might feel getting out of bed one morning after hard work the day before.' Pat Taaffe, who came frequently to call on his old friend, describes him as 'stiff in his hindquarters.'

Kavanagh makes a firm point: 'He was not in pain. He was, if you can divide the definition, more *uncomfortable* than *in discomfort.*'

The Duchess travelling back and forth that spring of 1970 says, 'We were pretty despondent. We'd cod ourselves that sometimes he was a bit better, but . . .' She sighs resignedly, remembering the passing days. 'He'd go out for a few hours most days, and he'd lie down a lot. . .'

Johnny Kelly felt the strain. Pat Taaffe says, 'You've seen the house where Kelly lives at the end of the yard and where it looks. So Kelly was looking out of his house all the time down the line to Arkle's box. And if he didn't see Arkle's head out, he'd been wondering whether Arkle had got down and would never get up . . .'

The Duchess said, 'I'd just been over, and he'd been pretty bad. He'd been lying down and didn't easily get up.' She'd hardly gone back to Cheshire when Pat Taaffe called to visit his old friend. He came over with his daughter Olive who loved feeding Arkle apples and pears. The great horse was having much difficulty moving. Pat telephoned the Duchess and Maxie Cosgrove. 'I rang Her Grace and said, "You'd better come over." '

Maxie Cosgrove examined Arkle yet once more, and telephoned the Duchess. She made the last, hardest decision in Arkle's life, and flew over from Cheshire to say goodbye to him. 'In the few days since I'd seen him, he was very much worse.' When she went in to see him for the last time, he was lying down.

It was Sunday afternoon the 31st May, 1970. Johnny Kelly could not bear to stay with his horse, but went up to his house at the end of the yard and shut the door. He said, 'All through the years Arkle would trust you. He took all those injections, because he knew that we were doing it to him for his good. And so . . .' Five years later, Kelly bites upon his lower lip and his eyes blink quickly.

It fell to James Kavanagh, who accompanied the miserable Maxie Cosgrove, to give Arkle his last injection. The great horse went down in his box and went to sleep forever.

As sometimes happens in loving human relationships, Arkle's old friend Meg did not long out-live him. By the end of August she was buried beside him in their grassy grave. It is surrounded by a banked hedge of daffodils in the garden at Bryanstown halfway between their old stables and what is now called Arkle's Field. The stone above her grave reads simply '*Meg A Good Hunter*'. Above Arkle's, facing the rays of the southern sun, is an even more simple memorial. As befits the last home of the greatest steeplechaser of all time it just states his name.

ARKLE'S RACING RECORD

DATE	COURSE	RACE	DISTANCE	VALUE	WEIGHT	JOCKEY	PRICE	PLACE
Season 1961–62								
Dec 9	Mullingar	Lough Ennel Plate	2m 1f	£133	11.9	M. Hely-Hutchinson	5/1	3rd
Dec 26	Leopardstown	Greystones Flat Race	2m	£202	10.7	M. Hely-Hutchinson	5/1	4th
Jan 20	Navan	Bective Novice H	3m	£133	11.5	L. McLoughlin	20/1	won
Mar 10	Naas	Rathconnel H'cp H	2m	£202	11.2	P. Taaffe	2/1f	won
Apr 14	Baldoyle	Balbriggan H'cp H	2m	£387	10.1	L. McLoughlin	6/1	unpl
Apr 24	Fairyhouse	New H'cp H	2m	£742	10.5	L. McLoughlin	8/1	4th
Season 1962–63								
Oct 17	Dundalk	Wee County H'cp H	2m 1f	£163	11.13	P. Taaffe	6/1	won
Oct 25	Gowran Park	President's H'cp H	2m	£463	10.5	P. Woods	9/2f	won
Nov 17	Cheltenham	Honeybourne Ch	2m 4f	£680	11.11	P. Taaffe	11/8f	won
Feb 23	Leopardstown	Milltown Ch	2m	£461	12.11	P. Taaffe	1/2f	won
Mar 11	Cheltenham	Broadway Novices	3m	£1,360	12.4	P. Taaffe	4/9f	won
Apr 15	Fairyhouse	Power Gold Cup	2m 4f	£1,137	12.5	P. Taaffe	2/7f	won
May 1	Punchestown	John Jameson Gold Cup	2m 4f	£852	12.4	P. Taaffe	4/7f	won
Season 1963–64								
Oct 9	Navan	Donoughmore Pte	1m 6f	£287	9.6	T. P. Burns	4/6f	won
Oct 24	Gowran	Carey's Cottage H'cp Ch	2m 4f	£519	11.3	P. Taaffe	4/7f	won
Nov 30	Newbury	Hennessy Gold Cup	3m 2f	£5,020	11.9	P. Taaffe	5/2	3rd
Dec 26	Leopardstown	Christmas H'cp Ch	3m	£846	12.0	P. Taaffe	4/7f	won
Jan 30	Gowran	Thyestes Ch	3m	£899	12.0	P. Taaffe	4/6f	won
Feb 15	Leopardstown	Leopardstown Ch	3m	£1,671	12.0	P. Taaffe	4/7f	won
Mar 7	Cheltenham	Gold Cup	3m 2f	£8,004	12.0	P. Taaffe	7/4	won
Mar 30	Fairyhouse	Irish Grand National	3m 2f	£2,630	12.0	P. Taaffe	1/2f	won

DATE	COURSE	RACE	DISTANCE	VALUE	WEIGHT	JOCKEY	PRICE	PLACE
Season 1964–65								
Oct 29	Gowran Park	Carey Cottage Ch	2m 4f	£741	12.0	P. Taaffe	1/5f	won
Dec 5	Newbury	Hennessy Gold Cup	3m 2f	£5,516	12.7	P. Taaffe	5/4f	won
Dec 12	Cheltenham	Massey-Ferguson Gold Cup	2m 5f	£3,989	12.10	P. Taaffe	8/11f	3rd
Feb 27	Leopardstown	Leopardstown Ch	3m	£2,583	12.7	P. Taaffe	8/11f	won
Mar 11	Cheltenham	Cheltenham Gold Cup	3m 2f	£7,986	12.0	P. Taaffe	30/100f	won
Apr 24	Sandown	Whitbread Gold Cup	3m 5f	£8,230	12.7	P. Taaffe	4/9f	won
Season 1965–66								
Nov 6	Sandown	Gallaher Gold Cup	3m	£5,165	12.7	P. Taaffe	4/9f	won
Nov 27	Newbury	Hennessy Gold Cup	3m 2f	£7,099	12.7	P. Taaffe	1/6f	won
Dec 27	Kempton	King George VI Ch	3m	£4,634	12.0	P. Taaffe	1/7f	won
Mar 1	Leopardstown	Leopardstown Ch	3m	£2,475	12.7	P. Taaffe	1/5f	won
Mar 17	Cheltenham	Cheltenham Gold Cup	3m 2f	£7,764	12.0	P. Taaffe	1/10f	won
Season 1966–67								
Nov 26	Newbury	Hennessy Gold Cup	3m 2f	£5,713	12.7	P. Taaffe	4/6f	2nd
Dec 14	Ascot	S.G.B. Chase	3m	£2,823	12.7	P. Taaffe	1/3f	won
Dec 27	Kempton	King George VI Ch	3m	£3,689	12.7	P. Taaffe	2/9f	2nd

Index